# Getting to Grips with English Grammar Year 6

Charlotte Makhlouf

We hope you and your pupils enjoy using the ideas in this book. Brilliant Publications publishes many other books to help teachers. To find out more details on any of the titles listed below, please go to our website: **www.brilliantpublications.co.uk**.

**Getting to Grips with English Grammar, Years 1–6**
ISBN:  Year 1:  978-1-78317-215-3
　　　　Year 2:  978-1-78317-216-0
　　　　Year 3:  978-1-78317-217-7
　　　　Year 4:  978-1-78317-218-4
　　　　Year 5:  978-1-78317-219-1
　　　　Year 6:  978-1-78317-220-7

Also by the same author is **Brilliant Activities for Reading Comprehension, Years 1–6**
ISBN:  Year 1:  978-1-78317-070-8
　　　　Year 2:  978-1-78317-071-5
　　　　Year 3:  978-1-78317-072-2
　　　　Year 4:  978-1-78317-073-9
　　　　Year 5:  978-1-78317-074-6
　　　　Year 6:  978-1-78317-075-3

Published by Brilliant Publications Limited
Unit 10
Sparrow Hall Farm
Edlesborough
Dunstable
Bedfordshire
LU6 2ES, UK

www.brilliantpublications.co.uk

The name Brilliant Publications and the logo are registered trademarks.

Written Charlotte Makhlouf
Illustrated by Paula Martry (GCI Illustration Ltd)
Cover design by Brilliant Publications Limited
Cover photograph: Teenage child enjoying climbing on a high rope course; Kzenon; (Shutterstock, Inc)

© Text Charlotte Makhlouf 2019
© Design Brilliant Publications Limited 2019

Printed ISBN:  978-1-78317-220-7
ePDF ISBN:  978-1-78317-227-6
First printed and published in the UK in 2019
10 9 8 7 6 5 4 3 2 1

The right of Charlotte Makhlouf to be identified as the author of this work has been asserted by her in accordance with the Copyright, Designs and Patents Act 1988.

Pages 15–83 may be photocopied by individual teachers for class use, without permission from the publisher and without declaration to the Copyright Licensing Agency or Publishers' Licensing Services. The materials may not be reproduced in any other form or for any other purpose without the prior permission of the publisher.

# Contents

Introduction ............................................................................................................................. 5
Cross-curricular Activities ................................................................................................. 6–14

**Theme 1 – Man-eating Shark!**
Man-eating Shark! ..................... Comprehension/hyphens ........................................ 15
Ambiguous Headlines ................ Hyphens ................................................................. 16
Twycombe Bay Match ............... Hyphenated words ................................................. 17
Derek's Diner ............................. Noun phrases ......................................................... 18
Shark Expert .............................. Noun phrases/fronted adverbials ..................... 19–20
Seals Attacked! ......................... Fronted adverbials ................................................. 21
'Great White Attack' by Melisande Green
 .................................................. Ellipses .................................................................. 22
Man Eating Shark Comic Book ... Ellipses/writing activity ......................................... 23
Mini Quiz .................................................................................................................... 24

**Theme 2 – Celebrity Gossip**
Celebrity Gossip ........................ Comprehension/semi-colons ................................. 25
Tammy's Diary ........................... Semi-colons ........................................................... 26
Celebrity Wedding ..................... Semi-colons ........................................................... 27
Chatkins Magazine .................... Semi-colons ........................................................... 28
Poochie Pampering Parlour ....... Subject and object ................................................. 29
On the Set ................................. Subject and object ................................................. 30
On the Set with Colin Creepe .... Clauses/semi-colons .............................................. 31
Celebrity Football Autobiography .. Colons .................................................................. 32
ROSCA Speeches ..................... First, second and third person ............................... 33
Autobiographies ........................ Writing activity ....................................................... 34
Mini Quiz .................................................................................................................... 35

**Theme 3 – The Chocolate Factory**
Behind the Scenes .................... Comprehension/synonyms and antonyms .............. 36
Chocco Chocolates ................... Synonyms and antonyms ....................................... 37
In Hot Chocolate! ...................... Synonyms and antonyms ....................................... 38
Chuck Chocbots! ....................... Proofreading and improving writing ....................... 39
Chocolate Dash ......................... Dashes ................................................................... 40
Pop the Chocolate in the Box .... Parts of speech ...................................................... 41
Packaging Problems ................. Parts of speech ...................................................... 42
Chocbots' Chocolate Sort-out! .. Suffixes .................................................................. 43
Robot Trials ............................... Word families ......................................................... 44
Cafeteria Complaints and Comments .. Linking ideas across paragraphs .................... 45
Production Lines ....................... Paragraphs/writing activity .................................... 46
Mini Quiz .................................................................................................................... 47

## Theme 4 – Dogwellan Lighthouse

| | | |
|---|---|---|
| The Haunted Lighthouse | Comprehension/formal and informal writing | 48 |
| Haunted Happenings at Dogwellan | Formal and informal language | 49 |
| Dogwellan Lighthouse Visitors' Centre | Formal and informal language | 50–51 |
| Leechwell's Manuscript | Subjunctive | 52 |
| Horatio Leechwell's Poetry | Subjunctive | 53 |
| Visiting the Dogwellan Lighthouse | Question tags | 54 |
| Plotting at the Smuggler's Arms | Question tags | 55 |
| Contraband Calamity | Question tags | 56 |
| The Legend of Dogwellan Lighthouse | Legends/writing activities | 57 |
| Mini Quiz | | 58 |

## Theme 5 – The Wobbly Flower Show

| | | |
|---|---|---|
| The Wobbly Flower Show | Comprehension/colons | 59 |
| Colon Capers | Colons | 60 |
| Cookery Demonstrations and Dog Trials | Semi-colons | 61 |
| Wobbly Contestants and Helpers | Active and passive voice | 62 |
| Wobbles at the Wobbly Flower Show | Active and passive voice | 63 |
| Flower Show Headlines | Active and passive voice | 64 |
| Dog Trials | Homophones | 65 |
| Village Fête | Homophones | 66 |
| Contestant Interviews | Punctuating speech | 67 |
| Wobbly Judges | Punctuating speech | 68 |
| Wobbly News | Writing activity | 69 |
| Mini Quiz | | 70 |

## Theme 6 – Pinkton-on-Sea

| | | |
|---|---|---|
| Pinkton-on-Sea Newspaper | Comprehension/layout devices | 71 |
| Pinkton-on-Sea Newspaper Planning Meeting | Layout devices | 72 |
| History of Pinkton-on-Sea Bandstand | Headings and subheadings | 73 |
| Seagulls | Subheadings | 74 |
| Pinkton-on-Sea Supermarket Wars | Columns | 75 |
| Pinkton-on-Sea Advertising | Punctuating bullet points | 76 |
| News Station Broadcast Notes | Bullet points | 77 |
| Pinkton-on-Sea Whales | Apostrophes for contraction | 78 |
| Proofreading Problems | Apostrophes for possession | 79 |
| Letters to the Editor | Apostrophes for possession | 80 |
| "No" to New Supermarket | Apostrophes | 81 |
| Pinkton-on-Sea Carnival | Layout devices/writing activity | 82 |
| Mini Quiz | | 83 |

Answers .................................................................................................................. 84–94

# Introduction

Grammar is important because it is part of our everyday communication. It helps us to be understood and to make our communication more effective, clear and powerful. It is a tool through which we can express ourselves. Teaching grammar effectively can give children the confidence to develop their skills much faster. It is believed to develop:

- attention and concentration
- language comprehension
- expressive skills
- reading and writing
- storytelling
- thinking skills

For those children for whom English is a second language, or for those who might be learning a new language, proper grammar is essential as all languages follow grammatical patterns. Grammar develops a skill for life, which flows into all areas of their lives. Future jobs may very well be dependent on the ability to communicate thoughts or ideas effectively, or present information logically and coherently.

Sadly, however, many of our grammar experiences are viewed as tedious. Many exercises are just pages of drills and the concept of grammar as being fun or exciting is eradicated. These books are designed to give children more confidence with their grammar. They have a range of exciting themes, filled with imaginative ideas, which will transport children through a grammatical journey that is fun and action-packed.

The comprehension activities at the beginning of each theme serve two purposes: they help to set the context for the activities that follow and they introduce key grammatical concepts. These activities demonstrate how grammar is used in context and provide excellent talking points for introducing and reinforcing the grammatical point being studied.

Within each theme there are opportunities for expanding children's writing. These activities are useful for assessing whether children can transfer the grammar points they have learned into their own writing. Mini quizzes at the end of each theme are designed to 'test' how much they have remembered.

Within each class there will be a variety of abilities. Less able pupils may need to have the instructions read and discussed with them prior to doing the activity. The Challenges at the bottom of each page allow more able children to be stretched and provide activities for faster finishers.

The books are linked to the requirements of the National Curriculum of England, where a knowledge of the correct terminology is also implicit.

Help your pupils get a firm grip on grammar and punctuation with this photocopiable six-book series, *Getting to Grips with English Grammar* for Years 1–6!

# Cross-curricular Activities

For children to gain a firm grasp of grammar and punctuation, it is important that the skills are not just taught in isolation; they need to be practised and reinforced across the curriculum. The chart below provides suggestions for how key grammar skills introduced in this book can be reinforced through different curriculum areas. Some of the History and Geography activities relate to topics in the National Curriculum for England.

| Grammar skill | Cross-curricular activity |
| --- | --- |
| **Hyphens** | **English** <br> In groups or pairs, use the following hyphenated words in sentences of your own to show how they can be ambiguous without the hyphen: world-famous, accident-prone, close-up, in-depth, funny-smelling, long-winded, sky-blue, bad-tempered, self-esteem, get-together, re-sign, re-form, baby-faced, well-known. <br><br> **English** <br> Make up some different ambiguous headlines (Man-eating Shark, see page 15), print them out on paper so that they are big and bold and use them as part of a class display. Use questions to invite other classes to suggest where the hyphens could go. <br><br> **English** <br> Make up a game or puzzle to help teach a younger year about hyphens. They could have a matching game to pair up the words correctly. |
| **Noun Phrases** | **Geography and Drama** <br> Imagine that Twycombe Bay is in the news again. This time ancient fossils, belonging to some dinosaurs, have been discovered. Use the following words and expand them using adjectives: fossils, shells, dinosaur, brontosaurus, sauropod, leaves, plants, cliff face, rocks, archaeologists. (You can use words of your own as well.) Then create an interesting and exciting news report about the discovery. You could act it out. <br><br> **English** <br> Sly Williams (Shark Expert, see page 19) is surveying the waters at Twycombe Bay. He thinks he has seen a new species of shark. Can you help him write up a new report about his findings using expanded noun phrases. You could also add subordinate clauses to improve your writing further and give more detail. |
| **Ellipses** | **English** <br> Melisande Green is planning another ending for her book 'Great White Attack' (see page 22). She is having difficulty with the ending and wants it to be a cliffhanger. Can you come up with some suitable endings each of which should end with an ellipsis. <br><br> Look at some modern books and find examples of ellipsis. Discuss how it has been used and the effect it has on the reader. |

## Cross-curricular Activities

| | |
|---|---|
| **Ellipses continued** | **Geography**<br>Research some unusual creatures/birds that we don't hear much about (which are real). Find out some facts about them and then use ellipses to portray those facts for different effects: omission of words, effect, trailing off into silence. For example: In a pride take over, all the youngest lions are killed … all of them. |
| **Semi-colons** | **English**<br>Celebrity Wedding (see page 27) – Make up two new characters for a celebrity wedding. Use semi-colons to say what they would like their wedding to be like.<br><br>Create a pet pampering parlour of your own for dogs (page 29). What will the gossip amongst the dogs be like at this parlour? Draw/paint some different dogs, give them names and then use speech bubbles to write what they might be saying. Use semi-colons to link your phrases.<br><br>Design a new tavern for the smugglers to relax in and discuss their latest plans (see page 55). What would it be called? You could plan an exciting menu for the smugglers – use speech bubbles to show the smugglers discussing what they might have in the menu, add semi-colons to link the phrases. For example: We could have seaweed stew; that's a healthy option.<br><br>**Geography**<br>Create a map of the area in which the smugglers work (see pages 48–58). You could tea stain it to make it look old and rip it up at the edges. The map should show all the different inns and taverns where they meet scattered around. You could add some islands too. Label the map. Describe specific features and use semi-colons to link your phrases. For example: This is Old Jim's Tavern; he's the one who lost his leg to the giant squid! |
| **Subject and Object** | **English**<br>Tako Takopolous (see page 29) is launching a new 'Glitter' store. He is giving a statement about it to the press. Can you write 6 statements for him which describe the store and how exciting it is? Make sure that you highlight the subject and object in each statement. You could use a different colour for each.<br><br>Imagine that you are Gloriella Bimbella (see page 30) OR her co-star Grog Stenburger. They are both keeping a diary of everything that happens on set, hoping that when it is finished they will be able to sell their stories to the press or turn them into a book! Make a list of all the awful things which have gone wrong as well as some great things that have gone right. Again, colour the object and subject of each sentence in a different colour.<br><br>**Drama**<br>Imagine that you are Gloriella's Mum or Dad. You are giving an interview to the press. Someone can play the part of the press reporter interviewing them. Make up questions to ask Gloriella's Mum or Dad. They should be answered in role! For example: Aren't you worried Gloriella could get hurt whilst filming? |
| **Clauses** | **English**<br>Create a celebrity magazine of your own. Give it a name.<br>Then produce an interview with Colin Creepe (page 31) in which you use semi-colons to show where the boundary is between the independent clauses. You could work with a friend. Think about what you would like to find out from Colin. How do you think he might answer it? |

## Cross-curricular Activities

| | |
|---|---|
| **Colons** | **English**<br>Write a celebrity autobiography (see page 34) of your own as an imaginary celebrity. Use colons to separate your independent clauses. Make sure the second clause gives a little bit more information about the first.<br><br>**History**<br>Do some research on a real celebrity who interests you. Find out more about their life and then select specific information and put it into clauses. Separate the clauses using colons. Perhaps you can present your information in the form of a poster fact file. You could use the posters in a class display.<br><br>**Drama**<br>Take on the role of another person. It can be anyone. Pair up with another person in the group. Have a conversation in which the first person starts with a clause and the second person has to imagine that they are completing the sentence with a second clause. The pause between you will be like having a colon to emphasise the second clause. For example: I played snooker last week: the cue snapped in half. How long can you keep it going? Who can have the best conversation? |
| **First, Second and Third Person** | **English and Drama**<br>ROSCA speeches (see page 33)<br><br>Create some speeches of your own for some new celebrities, using first, second and third person for them. Then act them out.<br><br>**Geography**<br>Plan out what the layout of the Chocco Chocolates Factory looks like (see page 36). You could draw a map of it and label all the specific features, for example, packaging room, manufacturing room etc. Imagine that you are giving a guided tour of the factory for the radio, use second person to give the guided tour. For example: You need to go to the packaging room where you see…<br><br>**Speaking and Listening/Drama**<br>Using your plan from above, imagine that you are a spy who has infiltrated Chocco Chocolates to try and steal one of the robots. Use the first or second person to describe where you are and what you are doing. You could get a friend to direct you as though they are masterminding the action from outside the factory. For example: "I am on the factory floor, to my right is the …" "You need to take the lift to the 2nd floor. On your right you will see …" |
| **Synonyms and Antonyms** | **English and Art**<br>Create some large posters to advertise the new chocolate products you have designed (see page 46). Use punchy words to describe your brand and add some cool pictures.<br><br>**Art/English**<br>Draw a large picture of a robot and paint it. Inside its tummy you could write a speech for it that you think it might be saying to welcome visitors to the factory. Turn it into a negative speech as though the robot has malfunctioned. Underline all the words that are negative and get a friend to suggest alternative antonyms which are positive. For example: Welcome to Chocco Chocolates, we hope you have a horrible tour. |

# Cross-curricular Activities

| | |
|---|---|
| **Synonyms and Antonyms continued** | **Media**<br>Prepare a television advertisement to promote your new chocolate products.<br><br>Prepare an advertisement for a new chocolate product and use negative vocabulary to describe it. Ask a friend to re-do the advertisement and find an antonym for all your negative words. For example: Buy Jellychocs – disgusting, foul-tasting treats with a repulsive jelly centre.<br><br>**Geography**<br>Imagine that the Haunted Lighthouse is going to be featuring in a new programme about lighthouses around the British Isles. Describe the haunted lighthouse (page 48). Highlight each adjective you use and then rewrite the article again changing the existing adjectives to a synonym. |
| **Editing and improving writing** | **English**<br>Gloriella Bimbella – write a piece for her diary and ask a friend to improve/add to it and correct it (see page 30).<br><br>**History**<br>Write an historical account of smuggling. Check it through with a friend to improve and edit it. |
| **Dashes** | **English**<br>In pairs and using a timer, take it in turns to write an opening clause, add a dash, the other person then has to add the next clause to close the whole sentence. How many can you do in one/two minutes? For example: Person One writes: Colin ate the chocolate quickly – Person Two has to end with another clause which relates to the first. For example: – which made him feel sick!<br><br>**History**<br>Research more about the history of chocolate – where it comes from and who discovered it. Write up your facts using dashes to separate your independent clauses. How many can you use?<br><br>**Art/English**<br>Design a class cafeteria (page 45). Invent some people and draw/paint them so they are nearly life size. You could put them on a classroom wall. Use speech bubbles that are really big and write gossipy comments you think they might be saying about the Chocco Chocolates Factory, using dashes to separate your two clauses. For example: Marlene's in hospital now – did you know her leg's broken! |
| **Parts of Speech** | **DT/Art/English**<br>Design a 2D machine on paper or card, which can sort sentences so that each part of the sentence is in its correct compartment. For example: all the nouns are sorted into a noun box/area, all the adverbs, verbs etc are sorted into their correct areas. A bit like a maths function machine only for sentences, so that when the sentence goes in all the words can be sorted.<br><br>**English**<br>Go around the class and each person has to make up a silly sentence. This sentence is then passed to the next person who has to sort all the words from the sentence, into a grid labelled with all the different parts of speech. |

## Cross-curricular Activities

| | |
|---|---|
| **Parts of Speech** | **Geography**<br>If you are doing a particular topic, for example, volcanoes, you can draw or paint a large volcano and then put all the different adjectives you can think of to describe it, in little boulders coming out of it. You could make a bank of important nouns to do with volcanoes and put them in a big 2D sack shape/vulcanologist beside it. You could have the vulcanologist saying something in a speech bubble and each part of speech from what they say can be sorted. The words could be put onto velcro and changed daily so it is interactive. For example: Inside the volcano the magma bubbles ferociously. Each of these words could be on a piece of card which is attached to the display (inside a speech bubble) and then the children could sort each word into the correct parts of speech boulder/box/sack/container on the board. |
| **Linking Ideas across Paragraphs Proofreading and improving your work** | **English**<br>What Melvyn Drubble does not realise (see page 39) is that some of the employees have been spying on him! They have had his phone tapped and all his conversations are being monitored! He has just had a long conversation with Symon Sneakle, his Production Manager. Symon Sneakle is very keen to use robots because they don't answer back to him like humans. In their secret conversation they talked about a variety of things: the importance of A.I., his new chocolate idea (you could make this new idea up), new compostable packaging, driverless lorries. In pairs or small groups, imagine that you are Melvyn and Symon and write out the conversation in detail, using paragraphs to link the ideas to show a shift in location, mood, viewpoint or new speaker. Act out the conversations in a Drama lesson.<br><br>How do you think the factory workers might respond to this conversation? Make up some new cafeteria complaints and comments to show how they feel about this secret discussion. Check your work carefully. Edit it where appropriate.<br><br>Design the front cover of what you think Chatkins Magazine might look like (see page 28). Use specific layout devices to make your work stand out and look effective and attractive. Write an article for the magazine using paragraphs to help you to separate the information. With a friend, improve and amend what you have written. Look carefully at the words you have used and see if an alternative synonym/antonym could be used which is better.<br><br>**Geography**<br>Research different magazines around the world. Find pictures of their front covers and then display where they are located around the world on a large map. |
| **Formal and Informal Language** | **History**<br>Imagine you could have a conversation with a famous person in History or Science. Write down what you think you might say to them and what they might say back, using informal language. Now imagine that you are a famous King or Queen addressing your subjects on a formal matter (you can make one up). Use formal language to address your subjects. |

# Cross-curricular Activities

| | |
|---|---|
| **Formal and Informal Language continued** | **English**<br>Write a couple of chapters for the new guide book (see page 49) using formal language. You can make up some quotes from imaginary people and put them into your guide book. Add illustrations to improve it.<br>Imagine that you are one of the King's Men. Write a report, in formal language, describing how you captured one of the smugglers. |
| **Subjunctive** | **English**<br>Lori has also found some interesting evidence that Captain Leechwell had a sweetheart to whom he wrote many interesting letters about his adventures (see pages 52–53). Imagine that you are Captain Leechwell – write a letter to your sweetheart about an exciting adventure you have had, using the subjunctive 'If I could … ' and 'If I were … '<br><br>**Poetry**<br>Write a poem using the subjunctive to highlight your dreams and aspirations.<br><br>**Comic Strip**<br>Design a comic strip for someone who aspires to be a superhero/footballer/Olympic athlete – you can choose – and use the subjunctive to write down what they could do or 'If I were … '<br><br>**Sport**<br>Analyse a game of football/hockey/tennis (you choose) that you have played. Use the subjunctive to comment on what you have done and how you could improve your next game. For example: If I were to practise my serve, I might improve my tennis game.<br><br>**Design and Technology**<br>Design the Chocbot of the future. Use the subjunctive to comment on your work and how you will make the robot. For example: If I were to use card … OR If I could take this … |
| **Question Tags** | **Geography**<br>Make a map of your own showing all the places around the Dogwellan Lighthouse where the smugglers hide their contraband (see page 56). You can add other places on the map and features. Around your map, which you can make old by tea staining, you can put lots of speech bubbles with questions from the smugglers asking where things are. Add question tags to the end of each bit of speech. For example: The lighthouse is near Clashing Rock, isn't it?<br><br>**Drama**<br>Imagine that you are pirates and you are planning your next smuggling expedition (see page 55). Keep the conversation going by making a comment and then adding a question tag to the end of the comment. Everyone has to keep the conversation going. The first person to forget the question tag, or who hesitates for too long, is out! |
| **Active and Passive Voice** | **English**<br>Prepare a commentary to give over the loudspeaker at the Wobbly Flower Show, in which you describe what is going on at the show, using the active and passive voice (see pages 62–64). For example: Sally's pony Daffodil, has just bolted out of the arena! (active) How many statements can you make? You could ask a friend to translate them – turn the active to passive sentences and the passive to active sentences. Does it make a difference to the commentary? |

## Cross-curricular Activities

| | |
|---|---|
| **Active and Passive Voice continued** | **English**<br>Create some wobbles of your own using the active and passive voice (see page 63).<br><br>**History**<br>Captain Leechwell left some secret instructions for his men so that they would not get lost in the caverns. Using the active and passive voice, can you prepare a list of instructions to guide the smugglers out of the caverns safely. For example: The bats' cave should be on your right [active]. Go left where the markings have been drawn on the cave wall [passive]. |
| **Homophones** | **English**<br>Brainstorm some homophones of your own. Create a puzzle/game for a younger year group to help them learn about the words you have just brainstormed.<br><br>Create some gossip of your own using different homophones (see page 66).<br><br>**Art/English**<br>Design a poster to show the different homophones you have brainstormed. Use the words in short sentences to show their meaning and illustrate each. For example: The peace was broken by the loud tractor. A piece of cake dropped to the floor. Try and be imaginative!<br><br>**Computing**<br>Design a game using code in which a dog (or other creature) has to collect bones (or something else) with homophones on them. Points can be scored for the number of homophones collected. |
| **Punctuating Speech** | **Speaking and Listening/Drama**<br>Interview one of your friends in the role of Sly Williams (see page 19) about the shark.<br><br>Get a friend to write down what Sly says and then transform it into correct speech which is properly punctuated. You could then transform this into a newspaper report. You could also do a large picture of Sly Williams in the style of a photograph and put all his comments into speech bubbles around him and use this as part of a display. |
| **Layout Devices**<br>**Edit to improve your work** | **English/Art/Computing**<br>Create a different comic book for the seals (see page 23) instead of the sharks, looking at the attack from their point of view. Use speech bubbles, headings and subheadings to make your story clear.<br><br>**English/Computing**<br>Imagine that you are a news reporter writing for a newspaper – write an account of the incident outside the Okoko Club in which Colin Creedy hits a police officer. You can make up events. Write an account of what happened, you could work with a friend to use IT to present your newspaper. Use columns, headings and subheadings. Don't forget to use eyewitness comments and use speech marks correctly for them! |

# Cross-curricular Activities

| | |
|---|---|
| **Layout Devices continued**<br>**Edit to improve your work** | **English/Art/DT/Computing/Maths**<br>Celebrity Wedding (see page 27) Imagine that you are the wedding planner organising the wedding of Lenny and Gracie. Plan the wedding for them based on the information that you have been given. You will need to produce menus, invitations, costings (how much everything will cost) flowers, venue etc. You might have to do some actual research to find out what certain things cost. Check/edit/proofread your work. Ask a friend to help you.<br><br>**Maths**<br>When you have thought about the venue (even if it is made up) you could think about calculating the area and perimeter of the space you have got. You could then imagine you are receiving 10% or 20% or 35% off some of the things you are buying. For example: you might receive 25% off the chair hire. If it costs £200 to hire 20 chairs what will the new cost be? Different groups in the class could be allocated specific tasks for this activity. How will you present all your information effectively when you have it? Use headings and subheadings to present it properly. |
| **Bullet Points** | **Geography**<br>Imagine that you are going camping at Pinkton-on-Sea (see page 71). Produce a list of things you might need to take with you using bullet points.<br><br>The residents of Pinkton-on-Sea (see page 77) have become increasingly alarmed about the huge amounts of plastic washed up on to the beach. Use bullet points to list all the dangers of plastic on the beach to people and sea creatures, to give to the councillors of Pinkton-on-Sea.<br><br>**Geography/English**<br>The manager of the new supermarket is trying to reassure residents about the effect the new supermarket will have on the town (see page 75). Use bullet points to highlight all the good things it will bring to Pinkton-on-Sea and use bullet points to show all the negative effects it will have on the seaside town. |
| **Apostrophes for Contraction** | **Computing/DT**<br>Produce a game or puzzle using either DT or Computing or both, for younger children to play to teach them about apostrophes for contraction. You will have to research all the contracted words yourself.<br><br>**Computing**<br>Seagull Swoop<br>Use coding to try and make a game in which seagulls have to swoop down and catch words which are contracted and match them with their long version, for example: we've – we have. Points have to be received for all correct answers.<br><br>**English**<br>Play a game of snap in which you have to design and make cards with the contractions and their long versions on them. Players have to play the game as if it were a game of snap, only when a contraction matches its full version you could shout 'Contract'.<br><br>Write a very formal letter to someone important in which you challenge yourself not to use any contractions at all. Perhaps you could rewrite the letter using contractions and see what a difference it makes. |
| **Layout Devices continued** | |

## Cross-curricular Activities

| | |
|---|---|
| **Apostrophes for Contraction continued** | **English and Drama**<br>Pinkton-on-Sea Whales: when you have written your guided tour for Old Kenny (see page 78), you could act it out with a group of friends who could be the tourists. You need to think of some good questions to ask Kenny about the lighthouse and harbour. |
| **Apostrophes for Possession**<br>**Edit to improve your work** | **English/Geography**<br>Create an imaginary show of your own (see page 59). It could be done in pairs or as a group. Make a list of all the stalls which will be at the show and use apostrophes for possession to show to whom the stall will belong. For example: Sally's roses, Beryl's cookery corner. Make a map of the show ground identifying where all the stalls will be put so that visitors can find the places they want to visit quickly. You could even add a couple of rings for where various events will take place. Make up some events that will be in the main show rings.<br><br>**English/Geography/History**<br>Create some new places of interest for visitors to see around the Dogwellan Lighthouse (see page 54). Use apostrophes for possession to show to whom these places belong. For example: the smugglers' caves, Nancy's Donkey Sanctuary. Create a leaflet for tourists in which you add all these new places. Describe them in detail, add pictures and a map of where they can be found in the area. Edit, improve and amend your work to check that it makes sense. Use headings and subheadings to lay out your information carefully. |

# Man-eating Shark!

Read the passage below. List all the hyphenated words you can find, then find the meaning of them.

**Hyphens** – can be used to join two words together. This helps sentences make sense and avoid ambiguity. **Hyphens** between words save confusion.
For example:
A man-eating tiger.
Or A man eating tiger!

# The Daily Wash

## Man-eating Shark!

A surfer was left badly injured in hospital yesterday, when he was attacked by a shark off the small beach of Twycombe Bay, on the West Coast of Britain.

The young man was said to be paddling out to sea when tourists on the beach saw him struggling in the water. Twelve-year-old Barry Brown told reporters, "He was wide-eyed with horror and thrashing about wildly, shouting for help. I saw what looked like a fin. Then the surfer began paddling desperately towards us. The fin was really fast-moving. Close-up this huge shark's head reared out of the water. You could see its razor-sharp teeth! I was terrified and began shouting for help."

Other tourists helped to drag the surfer out of the water and raised the alarm.

Apart from deep cuts and bites on his legs and arms, the surfer is recovering in hospital.

The coastguard and marine experts, have begun a co-ordinated hunt for the shark which is believed to be a cousin of the Great White.

"It is very unusual for sharks to be in these waters," Marine Biologist, Dulcey Whitlow told reporters. "They prefer Australian or Florida waters. However, in-depth studies have revealed that there have been more shark attacks around Britain's coastal waters in recent years. Up-to-date reports show shark attacks are happening more frequently in European seas."

Although this recent attack has frightened locals considerably, coastguards urge calm. "We would like people to co-operate and stay close to shore when swimming. We are also remaining open-minded as to the nature of the attack, which we feel was a one-off! At present, we are co-ordinating our search around Twycombe Bay and the surrounding waters."

Imagine you are the surfer who has just been attacked by the shark. Write an account of your ordeal using the following hyphenated words. (Remember to look up the words if you don't know what they mean).

| | | | |
|---|---|---|---|
| in-depth | half-hearted | well-made | well-intentioned |
| self-disciplined | quick-thinking | pick-me-up | well-known |

*Man-eating Shark!*

# Ambiguous Headlines

> **Hyphens** - can be used to join two words together. This helps sentences make sense and avoid ambiguity. Hyphens between words save confusion.
> For example:
> A man-eating tiger.
> *Or* A man eating tiger!

The Daily Wash have some interesting headlines! They are missing some important hyphens to avoid them being ambiguous. Can you write the headline out again, putting the hyphen in the correct place? Explain what the headline means with and without the hyphen.

## The Daily Wash
### Making a splash with the news!

- Man eating shark
- Whale eating fish
- Film star in high rise flat scandal!
- Pig headed reporters annoy locals

## Challenge

Can you write three ambiguous headlines of your own and then explain what they should really mean!

# Twycombe Bay Match

Draw lines to match up words from the left-hand box to the middle box to make a new hyphenated word. Then write out the full word in the box on the right. The first has been done for you.

| heavy | baked | build-up |
| hard | tempered | _____ |
| wide | moving | _____ |
| tight | handed | _____ |
| even | hearted | _____ |
| long | lipped | _____ |
| fast | eyed | _____ |
| build | winded | _____ |
| half | up | _____ |

## Challenge

Now use each of the hyphenated words you have made in some sentences of your own about the recent shark attack in Twycombe Bay.

Man-eating Shark!

# Derek's Diner

> A **noun phrase** can be one word, or a collection of words within a sentence, that contain a head noun or pronoun. For example: a shark, a fish, my coat, our lovely dog.

There's gossip afoot at Derek's Diner in Twycombe Bay. The locals have been discussing the shark incident.

Colour the comments to identify the noun phrases. Remember, a noun phrase needs to have a noun and a word with it to modify it, such as an article (a, an, the), or a possessive pronoun (me, mine, our, their, etc.,). One has been done for you.

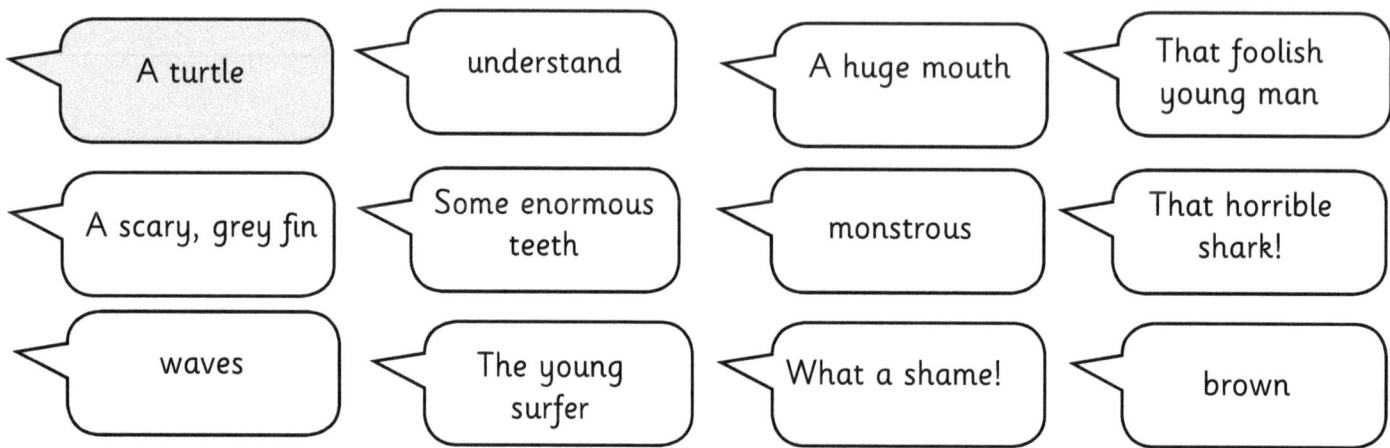

Can you find the noun phrases in these comments? First identify the noun (or nouns) in the sentence. Then underline the other words that are expanding it. The first has been done for you.

| | |
|---|---|
| I saw <u>a huge, grey</u> snout poking out of <u>the cold</u> water. | 'Snout' and 'water' are the nouns. |
| The poor, young surfer was on his ripped and battered surfboard. | _____ _____ |
| The hideous shark bared its ugly, rotted teeth before swimming away. | _____ _____ |
| He slipped on the slimy seaweed and we could see the terrible tooth marks on his poor legs and arms. | _____ _____ |

# Challenge

Colleen was an eye witness to the attack. She was with her dog, Bonnie. Underline all the noun phrases you can find in her statement.

> We watched the young surfer riding the big waves until he fell off his board. Suddenly, a huge fin rose above the water. I screamed "Shark, shark!", and he slithered quickly on to the board. I saw an enormous shark come out of the freezing water and circle the battered board. Bonnie growled and barked. Other frightened tourists ran forward to help the terrified boy get out of the water. His poor legs were badly bitten.

*Man-eating Shark!*

# Shark Expert

> A **noun phrase** can be expanded using adjectives.
> For example: A beautiful coral reef, a scary, old shark.

Sly Williams is a shark expert. He has been writing some information on the recent shark attack at Twycombe Bay. Can you help him improve his writing by expanding his noun phrases with some suitable adjectives. The first has been done for you.

<u>This horrible shark attack</u> has alarmed the small community of Twycombe Bay. Twycombe Bay is a _____ holiday place. It has _____ sandy beaches and _____ rock pools filled with _____ _____ crabs and other _____ creatures. The _____ tourists say that the _____ shark attacked the _____ surfer without any warning. After the attack, the _____ patrol boat was launched, but the _____ sailors on it said they had no sighting of the shark. My belief is that the shark is an _____ porbeagle shark which had lost its way from more tropical waters.

# Challenge

Your challenge is to expand the nouns in the boxes into noun phrases which you should then transform into sentences. The first has been done for you. Expand the nouns into a noun phrase with a determiner or article and then use adjectives to expand it further.

| shark   coral   seaweed |
|---|
| The terrifying, vast shark hid in the beautiful coral behind some dark, green seaweed. |

| lifeguard   children   beachball |
|---|
| _____ |
| _____ |
| _____ |

| teeth   fins   fish |
|---|
| _____ |
| _____ |
| _____ |

| speedboat   tourist   ice-cream |
|---|
| _____ |
| _____ |
| _____ |

| man   towel   sun cream |
|---|
| _____ |
| _____ |
| _____ |

| waves   current   wind |
|---|
| _____ |
| _____ |
| _____ |

Man-eating Shark!

# Shark Expert

> An **adverbial** is a word or phrase or clause which is used to modify a verb (or clause). **Adverbs** can be used as **adverbials**.
> **Fronted adverbials:** When an **adverbial** is used at the start of a sentence it is called a **fronted adverbial**. Fronted adverbials can indicate or describe the time, frequency, place, manner or possibility of something happening.
> After a **fronted adverbial**, there should always be a comma.

With the recent shark attack, residents and tourists have become quite nervous about swimming around Twycombe Bay! They have hired Sly Williams, the shark expert to find out more about this recent attack. Here is his account. Read his account and identify the fronted adverbials by underlining them. The first has been done for you.

Even though it was a bad idea, we set off around dawn in the boat. Before we knew it, the weather had turned really spiteful. Every so often, giant waves would lash the side of the boat. At Porter Point, we turned North, the strength of the sea pitching and rolling us fiendishly. To my horror, I saw a giant fin ahead of us. It was the shark. As the spray lifted, we could see the beast ahead of us. Although I was terrified, I turned the boat towards it. Fast as lightning, it sensed my presence and whipped around, swimming furiously for the boat. Almost immediately, the boat lurched and shuddered as its huge bulk slammed against the hull. Three times, the beast hurled itself at us, until I was terrified it would split the boat in two. At the back of the boat, Beryl and Tom prepared the giant harpoon. But before we knew it, the shark had ducked beneath the waves and vanished. For the remainder of that day, we trawled the area but there was no sign of the shark. Exhausted, we turned the boat for shore. The following morning, we left the harbour early, ready for a new search.

# Challenge

Use the following adverbials to continue the expert's account of the shark hunt. Then try and make up six adverbials of your own to add to the account. See if you can create three fronted adverbials which are similes showing time and manner. Don't forget your commas after your fronted adverbial.

| To our surprise ... | Keeping close to the island ... |
|---|---|
| Meanwhile ... | Under the seaweed ... |
| To begin with ... | As a result ... |
| Rarely ... | Grabbing the rope tightly ... |

# Seals Attacked!

> **Fronted adverbials** are words or phrases which come at the front of a sentence. They help to describe the action that follows. They can tell you more about where or when things have happened. There should always be a comma after the **fronted adverbial**.
> **Fronted adverbials** do not make sense on their own!

Roland Ragu has reportedly seen the shark attacking seals near Seal Island. Seal Island is not far from Twycombe Bay. Can you improve his report by adding fronted adverbials to his sentences? The first has been done for you.

<u>Early this morning</u>, I left the harbour in my small boat. _____, there was a good breeze. My plan was to sail around the bay to Midnight Rock. _____, I picked up Sally Barnes from the Lighthouse. _____, she's a fabulous photographer. We made our way around Shingle Sands and out towards Seal Island. _____, I've had my boat for twenty years! Sally was hoping to get some good pictures of the seals and cormorants. _____, we arrived near Seal Island. _____, we could see the seals playing. _____, Sally took a few photos. _____, we saw a huge fin rise out of the water! _____, I turned the boat towards the island. _____, the seals were really panicked! The waves boiled and foamed. _____, the shark burst out of the water. _____, it began chasing all the seals in the water! Sally and I watched in shock! _____, the shark grabbed one of the seals! _____, the seal was tossed into the air. We thought it was going to die! _____, the seal swam away back to the island. _____, the shark just vanished. _____, we waited for it to return. _____, the seals appeared to be nervous and jittery. _____, we made our way to Midnight Rock. _____, it was hard to believe what we had seen. _____, we reported everything to the coastguard who didn't believe us! Then we showed him Sally's photos.

**Fronted adverbials to help you.**
Sadly,
Today,
Yesterday,
Afterwards,
Occasionally,
Every second,
Before we knew it,
To our surprise,
Quite accidentally,
Quick as a flash,
Unfortunately,
North of the Island,
Under the waves,
Up in the sky,
As soon as we could,
Wherever we looked,
As fast as possible,
Before noon,
As the sun sank,

Imagine that you are the seal who was grabbed by the shark. Using fronted adverbials of your own, write a description of what happened and how you felt.

# Challenge

Imagine that you are a reporter on the Daily Wash. Write a report on this recent attack by the shark on the seal colony. You can be imaginative and add additional details of your own. Don't forget to use fronted adverbials, paragraphs, headings and subheadings for your report. You will also need to get some good eyewitness quotes – use Roland and Sally's report to help you and add details of your own.

Getting to Grips with English Grammar, Year 6
© Charlotte Makhlouf and Brilliant Publications Limited

*Man-eating Shark!*

# 'Great White Attack' by Melisande Green

Melisande Green has written a powerful, new novel called 'Great White Attack', strangely enough it is all about a Great White shark!

> **Ellipses** are the three dots used at the end of a sentence for effect or the build up of tension, or for the trailing off into silence. They can also show an unfinished thought or the omission of words. For example: 'He wished he had never gone …'

Here are some sentences from her book, in which she has used ellipses for a variety of different purposes. Can you identify which is which and using three different coloured pencils colour them accordingly. One has been done for you. Then, imagining that you are Melisande Green, write a sentence of your own for each of the three types of ellipsis, which will be included in her book.

| omission of words | pause for effect | trailing off into silence |

| The boat rocked gently on the waves and I waited … | Sandra get the … for goodness sakes' get it now! |
| I mean, it was a Great White … wasn't it? | And the result was … disaster! |
| I turned swiftly, behind me two eyes glittered … | It couldn't be true … had they really swum this far? |
| Quickly Brian … pay attention … yes, YOU, Brian! | "You are mine," he hissed menacingly, "all mine … " |

# Challenge

In these extracts from Melisande's book, can you decide where you would put the ellipses? You might have to remove some of the punctuation.

| For one moment time stood still, absolutely | We threw out the bait, literally threw it out, then we waited. |
| It was a stupid idea, really stupid, but it could work. | I weighed my choices and found there were none. |

# Man-eating Shark Comic Book

Using the story at the start, can you create a comic book strip to tell the events of the shark attack? Use pictures and text to tell the story. Don't forget to use the technique of ellipsis and create interesting noun phrases and expanded noun phrases.

*Man-eating Shark!*

# Mini Quiz

**A. Tick all the noun phrases.**

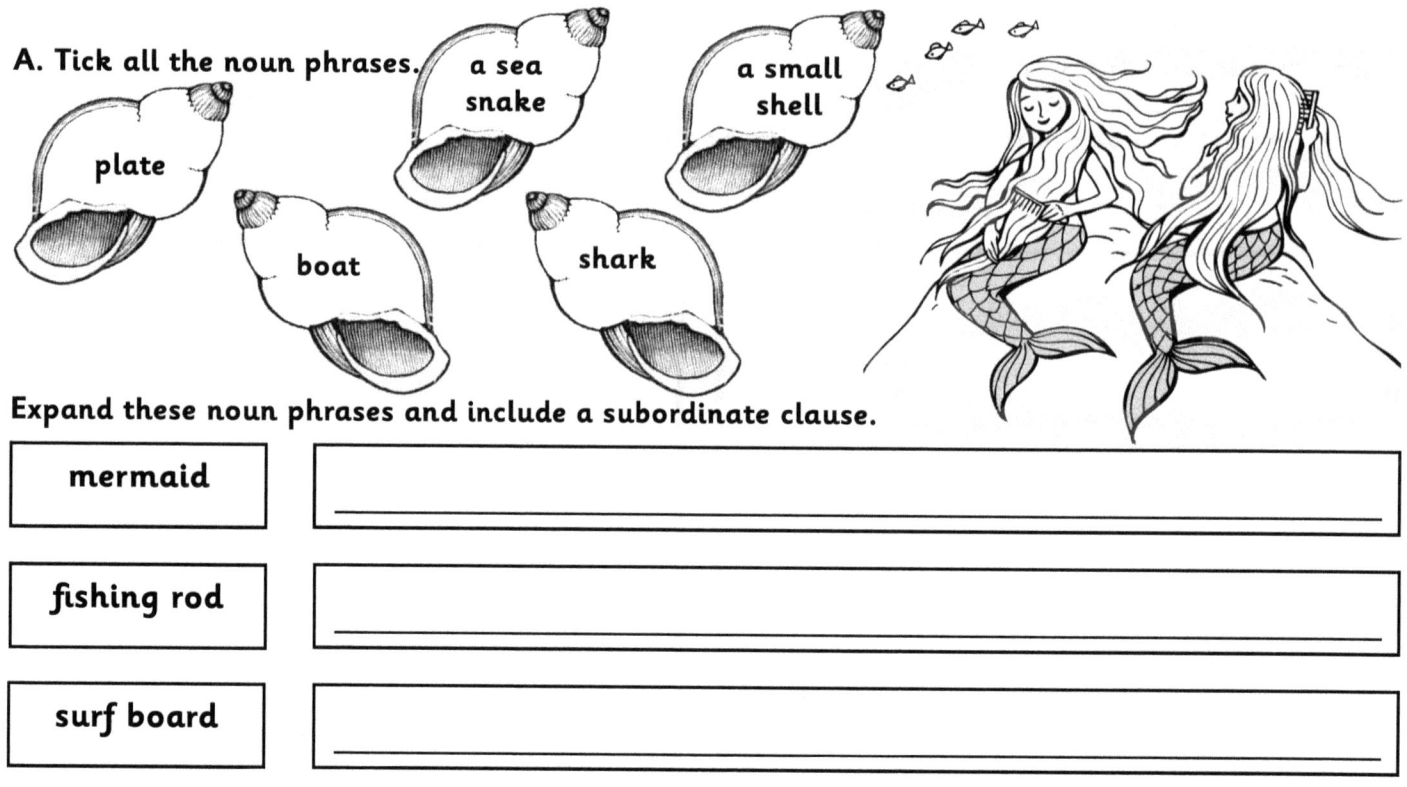

Expand these noun phrases and include a subordinate clause.

| mermaid | _____ |
| fishing rod | _____ |
| surf board | _____ |

**B. Put hyphens into these headlines so that they are not ambiguous.**

| A fish eating sea snake | Granny wins power driven motor boat. | It's a toy biting dog. |

| Two week holidays to be won! | A little used fishing boat for sale. |

**C. Rewrite these comments putting in the ellipses.**

1. Seriously, you went swimming when there's a shark out there?
2. Get out of the water, now!
3. It's coming for me, run!

_____
_____
_____
_____

# Celebrity Gossip

> **Semi-colons** are like commas or full stops, they are a short pause or little rest within a sentence. Full stops are the strongest pause, commas are the weakest pause, **semi-colons** are in between full stops and commas.

It is rare for celebrities to keep daily diaries, however, Gary Greengold, the actor, does keep a daily diary of all his doings! He's planning to turn it into a book one day!

Using a highlighter pen, mark all the semi-colons in the passage. With a friend discuss how they have been used and how effective you feel they are.

---

Thursday 15th November

    10.30am

    Simon missed his entrance again last night; the idiot! Luckily the audience didn't notice; which was a relief. Jackie and I stood on stage rabbiting on about next to nothing, until he came bustling on, sweating like a pig in his doublet and hose. You should have seen the look Jackie gave him; he almost forgot his lines as a result!

    Still waiting for my agent to get back to me about 'Twelfth Night'. I'm desperate to play the part of Orsino; what a challenge that would be! Auditions take place next week so Ursula needs to get in touch quickly.

    7pm

    Dame Edith Perkins is marrying again; for the fourth time! It was in the news and to that awful fizzy drink manufacturer, Kent Karbunckle. She can't be marrying him for love; must be the four yachts he owns and the flashy lifestyle. I remember when Dame Edith was merely Gwendoline Pratt; she changed her name pretty speedily when she had her blinding success in the film 'Cotton Buds'. Perhaps I should change my name?

---

Friday 16th November

    Ursula has been in touch; they want to see me! I'm spending hours rehearsing; let's hope the audition goes well and they call me back. It must be a good day because Ursula has got me a role in the new space adventure film, 'Bot Droid'. She says I shouldn't get too excited as it's only a walk on role; Yamoto Kimono is in it though! I'm such a fan of hers; she's an incredible actress. Yamoto is playing the role of the Bot Princess 'Yamdroid'; 'Yamdroid' gets rescued from the scrap yard by the Bot hero-down-and-out, Chungking. What wouldn't I give to play the role of Chungking!

    Tammy Ryder was here last night with her awful Pekingese dog, Poochie. Poochie yapped its head off the whole time; Tammy locked her in the kitchen. "Darling," I told her, "that dog of yours is a nightmare; so unsociable!" Tammy's going to be the new face of 'Lemonelle' beauty products; I nearly fell over when I heard what she's getting paid! Still, the hours are unsocial: it will be awful for her with those early starts ... crippling.

---

## Challenge

Write a short diary extract of your own to record your day so far. Use semi-colons to link some of your sentences and provide a pause.

Celebrity Gossip

# Tammy's Diary

Unknown to Gary Greengold, Tammy also keeps a diary! Here are some snippets from her diary. Can you add the semi-colon into each sentences to link the parts and provide a short pause? The first has been done for you.

> **Semi-colons** are like commas or full stops, they are a short pause or little rest within a sentence. Full stops are the strongest pause, commas are the weakest pause, **semi-colons** are in between full stops and commas.

Went round to Gary's place last night; what a shame he and Poochie don't get on.

I'm going to be the face of Lemonelle they are the top beauty product manufacturer!

Bonnie Tickler fell down the steps of the Okoko Club she broke her ankle.

Had supper with Raymondo Glass who rides an old motorbike I was wearing a short skirt so I couldn't get on it!

Colin Creedy hit a police officer outside the Okoko Club I don't think he's enjoying the cells.

**In this part of her diary, you need to put in FOUR semi-colons to indicate a short pause in the sentence.**

Went round to the offices of Lemonelle what an amazing building it is. Met Gerry Rainbow he's the photographer. We did a series of photos he wants to get an idea of how to shoot me. Had lunch with Mary Lolly she's got a new dog called Smoky.

# Challenge

**Can you complete the sentences?**

Colin Creedy didn't go to prison;
___

Lorna Crubb told the newspapers I'm marrying Gerry Rainbow;
___

Spoke to the Editor of the Daily Gleaner;
___

Smoky is adorable;
___

# Celebrity Wedding

**Semi-colons** are useful for linking two phrases where the information is similar. It is like taking a short pause which is not as strong as a full stop and yet not as weak as a comma. For example: Dennis was very good at hockey; he's bought some new shin pads.

Lenny Loudwater, the footballer, is marrying Gracie Gumble, who's a chat show hostess. They want the wedding to be perfect so they have got a wedding planner, Shaun Shakeup, to help them. Here are some of their plans ... add in the semi-colons.

I don't want the ceremony to be in a church an open air setting would be prettier.

Lenny doesn't want it to be too formal some people want to wear jeans.

I'd like the cake to be in the shape of a football there could be some small sofas around it.

We want an evening meal it will be a nice way to extend the day.

I'm keen to avoid wearing a white dress white always makes me look so drained!

I thought we could look at colour palettes colour will be an important part of your day.

## Challenge

Make up some comments of your own; use a semi-colon to separate your clauses. Don't forget to write the name of the person under the comment. The first has been done for you.

You might want to re-think wearing jeans; Chatkins Magazine will be there after all!

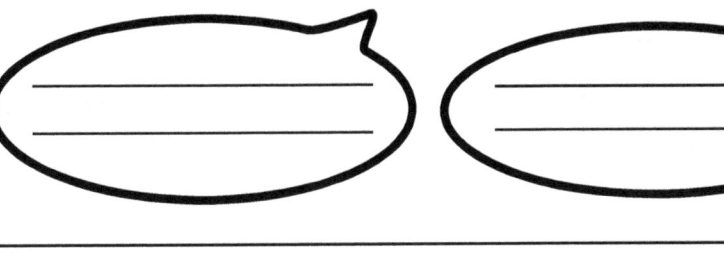
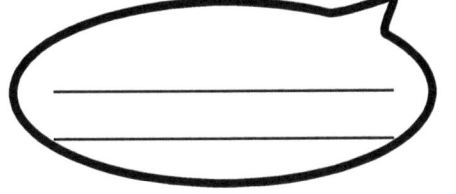
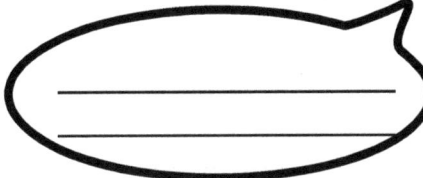

*Celebrity Gossip*

# Chatkins Magazine

> **Semi-colons** are useful for linking two phrases where the information is similar. It is like taking a short pause. However, sometimes when writing headlines more impact is made without them!

Chatkins Magazine has had a busy week. A lot has been going on in the celebrity world. Can you add a clause of your own to each of the following headlines, without adding a semi-colon. The first has been done for you (in bold).

| Frankie Floata's new film a Flop **Sales Drop!** | New Super Hero announced | Helga Rinkle marries Olaf Plunk |

Poochie Parlour Raided

Twinkle Brown trips on red carpet

**Now try writing the opening instead!**

| | | |
| could this be war! | will artificial intelligence take over? | hair dye sales soar! |

# Challenge

Can you write 6 headlines of your own for Chatkins Magazine. Then choose one of them and write an article for it.

1. 
2. 
3. 
4. 
5. 
6.

*Celebrity Gossip*

# Poochie Pampering Parlour

> The **subject** is usually the person or thing that the sentence is about.
> The **object** is usually a noun or pronoun, it is the person or thing that is receiving the attention.
> For example: Lenny (**subject**) stroked Poochie (**object**).
> The sentence is about Lenny and what he is doing, which is stroking Poochie!

Some celebrities' pets are getting some pampering at the Poochie Pampering Parlour!

They are also having a good gossip about their celebrity owner.

Highlight the SUBJECT in each sentence – green.

Highlight the OBJECT in each sentence – blue.

There might be more than one subject or object in the speech bubbles!

"Gwenda is going to marry Ted Brown, can you believe it?"

"Brian had far too much to eat and he was sick outside the restaurant – so shaming!"

"The paparazzi chased Tansy down the street!"

"Colin shouted at her. Then she threw him in the swimming pool!"

"The high heeled shoes landed on the pavement. The policeman helped to pick her up!"

"Des threw the guitar at the old woman. The old woman was furious and slapped him!"

## Challenge

Can you write at least SIX sentences of outrageous gossip that Buster has to say about his owner, Tako Takopolous, owner of the chain of jewellery shops called 'Glitter'. Highlight the subject of each sentence red and highlight the object of each sentence yellow.

Celebrity Gossip

# On the Set

> The **subject** of a sentence does the action to the **object**. For example: Benny ate the bananas. Benny is the **subject**. He is doing the eating. The bananas are the **object**, they are being eaten!

Gloriella Bimbella is filming on the set of her latest movie 'The Volcano Rages'. It's an action movie about a volcano obviously! The trouble is, filming is not running smoothly. Gloriella is talking to her mum on the telephone about all the different things that have gone wrong. Identify the subject and object in each sentence and highlight each of them with a different colour.

| Maybelle kept forgetting her lines! | Casper Craven's mask got stuck on his head! | One of the lights fell on the Director's caravan! |
|---|---|---|
| The heroine's dress snagged in the car door. | Sasha Grekorov's arm was broken doing a motorbike stunt! | Some of the cast got sea-sick on the boat going to the island! |
| Ogre Man's costume has been eaten by Douggie the Dog. | A terrible storm stopped filming for three days. | Douggie the Dog bit Kevin the cameraman. |

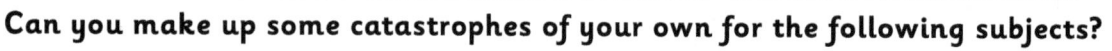

Can you make up some catastrophes of your own for the following subjects?

| Gerda Grenville, | the Director's car, |
|---|---|
| Kevin the Cameraman, | the makeup bag, |
|  | the exploding tree. |

# Challenge

Imagine that you are Gloriella's mum (or dad). Respond to each of her catastrophes with a sentence of your own. If there is a specific subject and object in your sentence, highlight them.

*Celebrity Gossip*

# On the Set with Colin Creepe

> An **independent clause** is one that can stand on its own. For example: 'The cat ate its food.' It has a **subject** and a **verb**. A **semi-colon** or a **dash** can show the boundary between two **clauses** which don't need a **conjunction** to join them.

Colin Creepe is on the set of his latest blockbuster 'The Dark Storm Rises'. He is giving an interview to Kev Smudgitt who is keen to find out more about the film. Add semi-colons to show where the boundary is between the independent clauses. The first has been done for you.

How's the film going Colin; I hear there have been some problems.

So it's got nothing to do with your leading lady she hasn't shown up!

I hear you're doing your own stunts isn't that very dangerous?

Oh that's just gossip as usual some lighting didn't turn up.

Shall we move on Kev Irina has just been delayed.

# Challenge

Can you add semi-colons to show the boundary between the two clauses, this time adding a clause of your own to finish off the sentence. The first has been done for you.

I trained as a stuntman; <u>there's a team of stuntmen to help me if I need it.</u>

The film sounds really action-packed

I hear this is your last movie

Now try writing two clauses of your own linking them with a semi-colon.

*Celebrity Gossip*

# Celebrity Football Autobiography

> **Colons** can be used to separate independent clauses, where the second clause gives a little more information about the first clause. For example: Johnny loved football: it was his favourite game.

Ollie Brentwhistle, the celebrity footballer, has released an autobiography of his life. He's been going through some of the pages and has been asked to put in some colons to separate the independent clauses. He's not very good at writing, can you help him? The first has been done for you. There may be more than one colon needed in some of the boxes.

| | | |
|---|---|---|
| When I was a kid I loved ice-cream**:** especially chocolate ice-cream. | My Mother used to be a ballet dancer she was amazing in 'The Nutcracker'. | I was signed up for the Tigers for two million pounds this is an unbelievable sum of money. It's an honour to play for the Tigers they're such a great team. |
| I was really useless at school I could hardly read and write. Then a guy called Bruce Goalie helped me he taught me to read and write. | At twelve, I was spotted by a local coach he was a really great influence in my life. It was at a match against Goddling Wanderers that my life changed this was my great breakthrough. | |
| I joined the school football squad when I was six we did a lot of matches. This really helped me become a team player you have to help your mates. | I'm really careful about my fitness and what I eat a healthy lifestyle is vital for my playing. | |

**Match the clauses, by colouring, to the one which is dependent on the other.**

| | |
|---|---|
| I met my girlfriend Polly in Spain. | It would be a fantastic achievement. |
| I'd like to help local kids play football. | She is really special to me. |
| My dream is to win the World Cup. | I'm going to have lessons at Christmas. |
| I have never learnt to drive. | They are the footballers of the future. |

# Challenge

Ollie has been asked to write about his famous goal against the Saltworth Rangers. Can you write some independent clauses to describe this amazing goal, using colons to separate the clauses.

_____

_____

_____

*Celebrity Gossip*

# ROSCA Speeches

> When we are writing we can use the:
> **first person**
> I, me, we, us, mine
> **second person**
> your, you
> **third person**
> they, he, she, it

Some celebrities have been preparing their speeches in readiness for the prestigious ROSCA Awards. It is doubtful that they will get a ROSCA Award, however, they are hopeful! Identify whether the speech is written in the first, second or third person, then write the corresponding letter in the correct award.

•1st person•

•2nd person•

•3rd person•

**A.** It gives me great pleasure to accept this amazing award. I am so excited. This is an amazing moment for me.

**B.** I don't know what to say … I'm so grateful … thank you to my agent, Drusilla and to Perkin … I love you both, you're beautiful!

**C.** You're the best Lula! You were always there for me … You can't believe how your support helped …

**D.** In a very lengthy ceremony last night, Benny Brown won the ROSCA for Best Actor in his film 'The Blue Aeroplane'.

**E.** … I love you Gavin … what a great director you are. It took us a while to make this film but we did it …

**F.** Wow! What can I say. This is a fantastic achievement for me …

**G.** You can't imagine how hard the team worked. Your whole day was spent shooting scenes …

**H.** … You have worked so hard and your inspiration is amazing. You are a true genius of film!

**I.** She burst into tears and clutched her ROSCA to her heart.

## Challenge

Can you write three more short speeches for first person, second person and third person. Then using the first person, imagine you are a famous actor/actress and prepare an acceptance speech of your own for the ROSCA you hope to win!

*Celebrity Gossip*

# Autobiographies

> An **autobiography** is a piece of writing which is all about the person writing it.

**Write an autobiography of your life so far. Write about all the things you have done. Don't forget to use all the different styles of punctuation you have learnt about to enhance your writing.**

_____

**Now make up an imaginary celebrity of your own. Write an autobiography of their life imagining you are that celebrity. What exciting things have they done?**

_____

# Mini Quiz

A. Celebrity Space Explorer Jasmine Starr, has returned from her latest mission to the ISS (International Space Station). She has taken some photographs of the world and written comments under them. Colour the subject of each sentence red, colour the object blue.

The storm raged over the Atlantic Ocean.

You can see a weather front swirling around Britain.

Can you see the pollution surrounding Russia?

B. Complete the sentence with another independent clause.

Billy tripped on the red carpet; _____

Lola and her dog Muffin were late; _____

Colin signed the autographs quickly; _____

_____; it had been a nightmare!

_____; the hotel was awful!

C. Complete the sentence with another clause that is dependent on the first.

I would never marry him:
_____

My life changed forever:
_____

We signed hundreds of autographs:
_____

Melvin was mobbed by his fans:
_____

_____
I was really furious!

_____
what a disaster!

*The Chocolate Factory*

# Behind the Scenes

> **Synonyms** are words which are different but have the same meaning, for example: cold – freezing. **Antonyms** are words which have the opposite meaning – for example: hard – soft.

Melvyn Drubble is the Managing Director of Chocco Chocolates. He is making his annual speech to the board, however, this year it is rather controversial!

Change the underlined words to an alternative synonym (word that is different but which means the same). You might need to use a Thesaurus to help you.

---

**Chairman's Speech to the Board of Directors of Chocco Chocolates**

Times are changing and we must <u>adapt</u> to meet them. Last year we developed three new brands which have been both popular and <u>lucrative</u>. We introduced two new wrapping machines, which have proved faster and less wasteful than our previous machines and we have <u>redeveloped</u> our flavours' room, putting in brand new work surfaces, machinery, mixing utensils, refrigeration and storage facilities. Though this was costly, we hopefully will see an improvement in our productivity and creativity.

Today I have a <u>controversial</u>, new proposal for you; I believe that this will benefit the Company enormously and reduce our costs significantly. The mechanical and digital age has exploded around us; it is increasing <u>rapidly</u>. Each year technology <u>expands</u> and improves and we must improve with it if Chocco Chocolates is to survive. Not only that, our competitors are expanding. We are in direct conflict with Dreamy Sweets; they have increased their product line and lowered the cost of their sweets, making them more affordable to the public.

I, therefore, propose that to reduce our costs dramatically and boost our public profile, we take the decision to bring in artificial intelligence to do the bulk of human jobs. I know that this will be a highly <u>radical</u> move, however, I also believe that <u>desperate</u> times call for desperate measures if Chocco Chocolates is to survive.

Thirty per cent of our production is already automated, we should now take the bold step of bringing it up to 60%, which will reduce our costs considerably. There will be no need for expensive salaries: robot workers do not require tea breaks, lunch breaks or rest breaks. There will be no need to pay them a salary or overtime and AI workers do not require holidays. This means we can keep productivity going both day and night.

We will of course, need a small number of people to deal with any AI malfunctions, however, I am confident that only a small percentage of time will be wasted on this. I also propose that instead of calling them 'AI Workers', that they are known as the 'ChocBots'. 'ChocBots' are the future. Let's <u>embrace</u> the future and reap the rewards.

---

# Challenge

Present an argument both 'For' and 'Against' the introduction of Chocbots. Before you begin writing your argument, write out at least three reasons why there should be ChocBots and three reasons why there should not be ChocBots.

# Chocco Chocolates

**Synonyms** are words which are different but have the same meaning, for example: cold – freezing. **Antonyms** are words which have the opposite meaning – for example: hard – soft.

Denzil and Delly in the Marketing Office have been preparing some advertisements for some new chocolates. Write out the advertisements again, changing all the underlined words for a suitable antonym, change all the words in bold to a suitable synonym.

**Chocco Bites**
Revolting, crispy, giant-sized snacks which will leave you **craving** for more. **Coated** in thin chocolate with a fabulous inner layer of stale, **squashed** strawberries, Chocco bites are the perfect way to **end** an evening.

**Chocco Bites**
_____
_____
_____
_____
_____

**Chunkers**
Feeling **decadent**, then get Chunkers, the chunky straight bar that can be dunked in cold chocolate for a **supremely** poor drink! The less you dunk further surprises are **revealed** as **different** flavours burst forth: caramel, vanilla, cinnamon and blackcurrant. Get Chunking!

**Chunkers**
_____
_____
_____
_____
_____
_____
_____

# Challenge

Create two new chocolate products for the factory. Then write out a punchy, exciting advertisement for them both. When you have finished, write the advertisements out again, this time altering some of the words. Decide which ones should be changed to antonyms and which ones to synonyms and then swap with a friend to see what new words they can come up with!

*The Chocolate Factory*

# In Hot Chocolate!

> **Synonyms** are words which are different but have the same meaning. **Antonyms** are words which have the opposite meaning.

**Roger Rumbold is one of the Directors for Chocco Chocolates. He is furious with Melvyn Drubble for suggesting they should get robots to take over making all the chocolates. In this playscript, change all the words in bold to synonyms. Change all the underlined words to antonyms. You may have to change or amend the playscript in places so that it makes sense grammatically. When you have finished, try acting it out with a friend. How does it sound? How could you improve it?**

Roger: (Happily) This is wonderful Melvyn! You can't possibly be **thinking of** using artificial intelligence to do all the **work**! It would mean the increase of hundreds of jobs!

Melvyn: (Angrily) Don't be **silly** Roger! It's a **brilliant** idea! Just think of all the loss we'll make!

Roger: We don't need to get **rid of** people, we need to **improve** our marketing! Dreamy Sweets have employed 60 more people for their factory because they're making more sweets.

Melvyn: (**Smirking**) Then they can employ some of ours when we **move over** to artificial intelligence!

Roger: (**Aghast**) Making our workers employed will bring us good publicity, Melvyn, have you **thought about** that?

Melvyn: Of course I haven't! The world will **applaud** my decision. It means we are **embracing** the technology of the future. Robots are of the past. We're moving **closer** to the past than Dreamy Sweets.

Roger: (Pleased) Our employees **need** these jobs, Melvyn.

Melvyn: We won't employ everyone, Roger. Obviously we will keep some people to **maintain** the machines. Certainly we will need the engineers to ensure the robots don't improve.

Roger: (Calmly) Melvyn … we need **better** packaging! We should reduce our marketing campaign. This idea of yours **worries** me deeply! The workers will be happy! There might be strikes!

Melvyn: (Furiously) Are you saying our marketing is bright and exciting? The old sweet range is awful! The trials have **shown** that children hate them!

# Challenge

Can you continue the script? What else do you think they will say to each other? Perhaps you could introduce a new director to the conversation. What will his/her reaction be?

# Super Challenge

In groups, discuss Melvyn Drubble's (Managing Director) plan to use only artificial intelligence in the factory. What do you think of his idea? Present an argument FOR and AGAINST his plans and then present it to the rest of the class.

# Chuck Chocbots!

*The Chocolate Factory*

> Writing can be changed and improved through **proofreading and editing!**.

The workers at Chocco Chocolates have heard about the new Chocbots (robots). Charlie Dellwit, the foreman, has written a letter to Melvyn Drubble to voice their concerns. Charlie is going through the letter to make sure it is all right but his friends have some queries. Imagine you are Charlie and answer their questions. Explain why you wrote what you did and what you will do to improve the letter.

*Should we have another paragraph here Charlie?*

_____
_____
_____
_____

*Does it need to be this formal at the beginning Charlie?*

_____
_____
_____
_____

Dear Mr Drubble,

We are very concerned to hear that the factory is intending to get rid of its workers and replace them with robots. This would mean the loss of over 100 jobs!

At the moment, you have a **very clever** workforce. To replace them with robots would cost the factory **a lot of dosh**! We think that people are far more useful than robots.

**We don't** believe that robots will be more accurate than humans. **We don't** think that robots will be able to give the personal touch to customers that humans give.

We would be grateful for the opportunity to have a **bit of a chat** with you so that we can discuss this matter.

**Gratefully Yours**,

Charlie Dellwit
Foreman

*Do you think we should improve the words and phrases (in bold) Charlie?*

_____
_____
_____
_____

## Challenge: Look at Mr Drubble's response and answer these questions

Why is the opening paragraph so short?

Do we need all these paragraphs?

It's not a very friendly letter, why is it so formal?

What do you notice about the connectives and how they link the sentences? Do you think they are effective?

Dear Mr Dellwit,

Thank you for your letter regarding our proposed idea of replacing the current workforce with robots.

At present, the company has no intention of replacing our employees with robots, although the idea of AI is currently being debated by the Board of Directors.

We value our workers and the excellent work they do in the factory, however, we live in a changing world and it is important that the company embraces new technology. Having robots would enable us to produce more chocolates much faster, therefore supplying our customers around the world with greater ease. This is something that we need to consider, especially when costs are high.

We are happy to have a meeting with you to discuss the matter further. Please contact my Secretary, Gavin, to arrange a time.

With Best Wishes
Melvyn Drubble

The Chocolate Factory

# Chocolate Dash

> A **dash** can mark the boundary between two **independent clauses**. It is like a small pause between the two. Both **clauses** have to relate to each other in some way. For example: The chocolate was really delicious – this was surprising!

The object of this game is to either start the sentence or end the sentence or write two clauses of your own. Players take it in turns. Both clauses need to be able to make sense on their own.

If you throw a 1, 3 or 5 complete one of the clauses that have been started for you.

If you throw a 2, 4 or 6 then complete one of the boxes that are empty.

If you run out of clauses for 1, 3 or 5, then add a new box at the bottom.

The first player to finish all their sentences properly (and imaginatively), is the winner! Good luck!

| Player 1 | Player 2 |
| --- | --- |
| The chocolate flooded the room | Marlene slipped on the chocolate |
| – it was a complete disaster | – really, you didn't know? |
| The order was enormous – | The new spices were amazing – |
| The box broke in half – | All the chocolates looked disgusting – |
|  |  |
|  |  |

# Challenge

With a friend, make up a game involving dashes and marking the boundary between two clauses using them. Perhaps the game can be about winning chocolates. The winner might be the one with the most chocolates.

*The Chocolate Factory*

# Pop the Chocolate in the Box

**Parts of speech**
noun, pronoun, adjective, verb, adverb, preposition, conjunction, interjection and determiner – these are all parts of speech.

Pop the chocolates in the right box. Then draw 2 each of your own for each box.

| Noun | Interjection |
|---|---|
|  |  |

| Conjunction | Adjective |
|---|---|
|  |  |

Chocolates: Aaah!, spanner, timid, and, apple, whoops, vicious, because, so, glacier, Oh no!

**Getting to Grips with English Grammar, Year 6**
© Charlotte Makhlouf and Brilliant Publications Limited

This page may be photocopied for use by the purchasing institution only

*The Chocolate Factory*

# Packaging Problems

**Parts of speech**
noun, pronoun, adjective, verb, adverb, preposition, conjunction, interjection and determiner – these are all parts of speech.

Nellie has tripped and dropped all the chocolates. Can you put them in the correct boxes? Cut out the pieces and stick them in the correct box.

| Noun | Pronoun | Adjective |
|---|---|---|
|  |  |  |

| Verb | Adverb | Preposition |
|---|---|---|
|  |  |  |

| The | delicious | sweets | melted | stickily | on | the | table. |
|---|---|---|---|---|---|---|---|
| The | evil | queen | drank | her | potion | noisily. |  |
| Under | a | boiling | volcano | the | dragon | slept | sweetly. |
| The | beautiful | bird | flew | happily | under | her | nest. |

# Challenge

Now write five sentences of your own and put each word in the correct box. Any words left over, make boxes for the correct parts of speech and put the words in them.

# Chocbots' Chocolate Sort-out!

**Suffixes** can be found at the end of a root word. They can either change or add to the meaning of the word.

More programming has been done so that the Chocbots can sort the chocolates.
Add the correct ending to complete the words below.

-ent    -ance    -ancy    -ant    -ial

| exuber_____ | palat_____ |
| placem_____ | resembl_____ |
| perform_____ | brilli_____ |
| import_____ | torrent_____ |

| belliger_____ | abund_____ | tru_____ | inf_____ |
| fac_____ | defi_____ | vac_____ | signific_____ |

## Now try these:

-tious    -cious    -ence    -ency

| curr_____ | confid_____ | frac_____ | cons_____ |
| ambi_____ | frequ_____ | ficti_____ | independ_____ |
| fero_____ | deli_____ | emerg_____ | innoc_____ |

## Challenge

Use a dictionary to find out the meaning of the words above that you do not know.

_____
_____
_____
_____

*The Chocolate Factory*

# Robot Trials

**Word families**
Some words are distinguishable because they may contain the same **prefix** to begin them or they may contain the same **suffix** at the end. They may contain a **root word** that is the same. For example: holiday, Thursday, mayday – these words all contain day at the end.

Chocco Chocolates are using some of the new Chocbot Robots in trials, to see how effective they are on the factory floor. At present they are working on programming their speech. Can you identify all the different word families within the robot's speech? There are four. Label each box with the name of the word family. Write all the words relating to that family in the correct box.

Good morning!
Welcome to Chocco Chocolates. I am the latest in a line of potential robots for the factory floor. My work will be highly influential as programmers are working to ensure I am effective. In the world of artificial intelligence, we are causing a lot of interest. I have a special programme which enables me to control two machines at once. I will be able to read complicated diagrams. It is unbelievable that this interesting, new technology will now be able to control a whole factory floor. My technicians believe I will be extremely valuable with the potential to increase profitability. I am also very likeable.
    I have interchangeable hands that are multifunctional. Recent diagrams have shown that I have a few superficial problems which will require minor reprogramming. Last night there was an interloper in the factory who was caught trying to steal confidential information about the Chocbots. He tried to interfere with the wires and panels on one of my Chocbot colleagues. Interim reports show that when I am completed, it will be crucial to ensure my plans are safe, so that we are not stolen by rival companies who feel we are highly desirable. Yesterday, we had an important visitor who is extremely influential. He has a large role to play in the industrial world and he was keen to watch the robots in action. He wasn't very social because he ignored all the humans. When I spoke to him he remarked how valuable we would be.

# Challenge

Brainstorm all the words which end with -tious and -cious. Using the words you have found, can you write a report of your own about one of the Chocbots. Say how important and interesting they are and how they have benefited the factory.

**The Chocolate Factory**

# Cafeteria Complaints and Comments

> **Paragraphs** are useful for linking ideas. They can show – a shift in time, a shift in location, a change of mood, a new viewpoint or a change of speaker. They make text easier to read.

The staff at Chocco Chocolate Factory have been airing their views during their tea break. Imagine that you are a secret spy for the Managing Director, Melvyn Drubble. Sort the information by highlighting it, according to whether it conveys a particular mood or viewpoint.

They want to get rid of all the workers and put in robots. Robots! What a cheek! They can't call their chocolates 'artisan chocolates' if they haven't been given the human touch!

This is just a chance for the factory to save money! Robots won't make better chocolates, they won't spot imperfect ones either – AI – Amazing Idiots, that's what management are!

I remember when the factory was a tiny, family run place. It prided itself on the personal touch, looking after its workers, helping people. Everything changed when Melvyn Drubble took over as MD!

Melvyn's not interested in people. He's only interested in money; the company is sacrificing the old values for new trends.

We ought to be embracing change – change is a good thing. Look at all the wonderful new medical technology we have and what about mobile phones? They've been fantastic when connecting families and friends.

## Challenge

Melvyn Drubble wants you to put all the complaints and comments together into a report for him. You have to report back on what everyone says, linking all the ideas carefully together in paragraphs. Use reported speech.

_____
_____
_____
_____
_____

The Chocolate Factory

# Production Lines

> When writing don't forget to use paragraphs with punctuation including plural parentheses and colons, full stops and commas.

Imagine that you are one of the employees of Chocco Chocolates.
Easter is approaching, however, you need a new theme! Rabbits and Easter eggs have not been selling so well and people are getting fed up with them. Come up with a new idea to produce in chocolate; then write a speech to present to Melvyn Drubble, to persuade him to produce your idea for Easter!

**My Brainstorm of Ideas**

**My Chosen Theme** (expand your ideas)

**My Speech to Melvyn Drubble**

# Mini Quiz

**A. Chocco Chocolate Factory is under attack by a rival company who are keen to take it over. Replace the words underlined with a suitable antonym, replace the words in bold with a suitable synonym.**

Fellow Directors,
The time has come for us to <u>decrease</u> our Empire!
Word has come of a <u>small, insignificant</u> factory, named Chocco Chocolates. They produce **magnificent** chocolates of **excellent** quality and **fine** taste. Chocco Chocolates will **improve** our own company which is facing financial **problems** and a lack of creativity. We should <u>end</u> talks as <u>slowly</u> as possible and consider **negotiations**.

**B. Write an appropriate synonym and antonym for the words given below.**

| word | synonym | antonym |
|---|---|---|
| tasteless | | |
| disappointing | | |
| delicious | | |
| furious | | |
| reward | | |

**C. Where would you put the dash between these clauses.**

| Mouthwatering, strawberry-butterscotch swirls the ultimate in taste. |

| Bring romance to your life with Hearties feel the love envelop you. |

| Marvellous morsels of chocolicious fun perfect for that dinner party. |

**D. Now make up your own independent clauses for these products.**

_____

_____

_____

_____

Dogwellan Lighthouse

# The Haunted Lighthouse

**Formal and informal writing** – we write **formally** to people we don't know. *Instructions*, *explanations*, *reports* and *formal letters* are examples of **formal writing**. We write **informally** to people we know well. It might be via texts or emails, letters to family and friends or postcards.

**Formal or informal? Write an 'F' or an 'I' in the boxes.**

---

Dear Mr Higgins,
    I am writing to thank you for allowing me to read the old documents relating to the Dogwellan Lighthouse.
    This information has helped me enormously with my research; I have now discovered information which confirms that Captain Leechwell did indeed have a connection to the Lighthouse.
    I would greatly appreciate spending more time in the old library, to investigate this matter further.
    Yours sincerely,
Lori Baker

---

LoriB@notmail.co.uk

Hi Lori, got your message – excited to hear you found it! I knew Captain Leechwell was smuggling along that coastline! Did you find any references to 'Old Skip'?
All the best Tim

---

Hi Tim, I can't believe my good luck. Turns out Captain Leechwell was a horrible man, who wrecked many ships for their goods.

---

    Father was out late again last night. I was told to keep to my room and close the curtains; I knew why. There was to be another 'consignment' that night.
    They thought I was obeying orders, but I followed them to the coast, hiding myself in one of the covered carts.
    They'd obviously lit the beacons, for they were burning brightly when I hid behind bushes at the top of the cliff. The wind was devilish last night – freezing cold, whipping the waves into a frenzy.
    The wrecked ship was floundering badly on the rocks, where it had been lured. I could hear the shouts of men on board and my blood ran cold. There'd be no sparing of lives this night, for you can't salvage goods from a ship on which people are already living. I pitied the poor fools aboard, hearing their cries for help dwindle as my Father and Captain Leechwell rowed their small boats to them and climbed aboard.
    I watched them work swiftly to load the cargo and then hide it ashore, in the secret caves concealed amongst the cliffs …

---

Sir,
I write to inform you that we have caught the smuggler, Captain Horatio Leechwell …

---

Dearest Polly,
Your Father is caught! I will be waiting for you to take you to a place of safety. Meet me …

---

# Challenge

Imagine that you are Mr Higgins, the curator of the Dogwellan Lighthouse. Write a formal letter back to Lori Baker, giving her permission to visit the library again. Don't forget to use formal language, paragraphs and punctuation.

# Haunted Happenings at Dogwellan

Strange things have been happening at the Dogwellan Lighthouse. An exciting new guide book is going to be written about the lighthouse and its smuggling history! Can you change the informal comments into formal language? The first has been done for you.

| Informal | Formal |
|---|---|
| I was scared out of my wits by the old lighthouse keeper showing up one evening, you know. He had a lantern. | I was terrified one evening by the appearance of the old lighthouse keeper who was carrying a lantern. |
| Frightened the life out of me when I saw the ole smuggler on the stairs! He were carrying a bundle and walked right through me! I saw men rolling their barrels up from the shore. When I turned back, they wasn't there! | |
| The old lighthouse's been haunted for yonks, since I was a kid. I've seen loads of people carrying stuff in and out and then they're not there! | |
| I were on me boat one night. 'Twere dark and grisly weather. Would've crashed onto them rocks if the lighthouse's light hadn't come on sudden like, and lit up the rocks. Reckon it saved me life! | |
| There are ace ghosts too. I was out late one night and would've fallen onto the rocks if something hadn't pushed me back! Felt like hands grabbing me, like! | |

## Challenge

Start the guide book. Think about which pieces of information from above, you would begin with. Perhaps you can think of some exciting, formal language of your own to add to the book to make it more interesting. Think about the layout of the guide book. What headings will you use? What other information can you add?

*Dogwellan Lighthouse*

# Dogwellan Lighthouse Visitors' Centre

A new visitors' centre and tea room have opened up beside Dogwellan Lighthouse, to try and bring tourists into the area. Decide whether the comments are formal or informal and then change each into its opposite. For example: if it's formal, change it so it becomes informal language.

> Wow!
> What a great place to visit! The kids 'n' I had a great time looking out over the sea. It was a bit creepy going round the lighthouse; you could almost feel the ghosts watching you!

> Dogwellan Lighthouse is a wonderful place to visit. The children and I had a very pleasant time looking out over the sea. Visiting the interior of the lighthouse was rather scary, however, you could almost sense the ghosts watching you.

> Welcome to Dogwellan Visitors' Centre! We hope that you enjoy your experience with us and find out more about the history behind Dogwellan's infamous lighthouse.

_____
_____
_____
_____

> The kids loved the themed smugglers' menu with all the food in mini barrels. It was really cool.

_____
_____
_____
_____

> There's a fab history behind Dogwellan! Captain Leechwell sounds dead scary, especially since he went round killing folks to get his booty. He even lit beacons to make ships crash against the rocks!

_____
_____
_____
_____
_____

> The staff are really great – helpful and friendly. There is even wheelchair access to help the elderly. You can get fab teas in the cafe which has really good grub!

_____
_____
_____
_____
_____

# Dogwellan Lighthouse Visitors' Centre

## Challenge

**Rewrite these customer testimonials in informal language.**

… what a delightful place to visit. We were greeted by your most friendly and considerate staff, for whom nothing was too much trouble. The food was delicious and the variety quite incredible. We thought the guided tour of the lighthouse was most informative and well-presented …

… we would like to thank you for your helpfulness. Our visit was a truly memorable experience, for which we are most grateful …

… it is difficult to believe that this beautiful coastline contained so many smugglers. I particularly enjoyed the coastal tour, which gave a huge amount of information describing the wicked exploits of Captain Leechwell. He sounded an interesting, although evil, individual. The children took great pleasure in dressing up as smugglers and recreating what it must have been like to hide in caves …

Dogwellan Lighthouse

# Leechwell's Manuscript

> The **subjunctive** is a **verb** form that is used to express things that could or should happen. It is also used to express wishes, hopes, demands or commands. For example: If I were Queen … or I wish I were going to Mars! It can make your text more formal.

Pieces of an ancient manuscript have been found belonging to Captain Leechwell. In it, the Captain talks to his men and makes proposals to them. Sort all the sentences into the correct columns. One has been done for you.

| Subjunctive | Non-subjunctive |
|---|---|
|  | I have a cunning plan to outwit the King's Men! |

1. The weather was vile but we had a good haul that night – plus three kegs of rum!
2. If I were in your position, I would think twice before speaking to me like that!
3. I am recommending that we tie lanterns to goats' necks and release them along the cliffs!
4. It will be imperative that she keep quiet!
5. When we arrived at the top of the cliffs, we could see the wrecked ship on the rocks.
6. I demand that we hide the goods in the caves.
7. I have a cunning plan to outwit the King's Men!
8. It took a while to hide the booty in the caves.
9. Fellow Smugglers, I propose that we use the full moon tonight to go wrecking!
10. I ask that you keep your daughter out of the way tonight!
11. I wish it were possible to defy the King's Men!

## Challenge

Then, write four sentences of your own, using the subjunctive which could come from the manuscript.

# Horatio Leechwell's Poetry

*Dogwellan Lighthouse*

> The **subjunctive** is used when we want to talk about things that could or should happen. For example: If only we were going to the seaside. OR If I were you I wouldn't do that!.

Lori Baker has returned to the Dogwellan Library where she has uncovered some strange pieces of parchment. It seems that Captain Horatio Leechwell has been writing poetry. Highlight all the sentences which use the subjunctive.

| | |
|---|---|
| Come fair or foul<br>Thy shining light beckons.<br>I wish we could turn the stars to gold<br>and flood the sea with silver.<br>If I were younger, I would risk the churn at Sharks' Rock,<br>But your wise light guides me away … | You demand that we go,<br>I pray that we stay,<br>My ship could not spare another day of endless turmoil.<br>Such feckless dreams<br>To sink my men's bones,<br>Where I wish they'll never go<br>In Davy Jones's locker. |

Lori has found these pieces of parchment.
Can you use the writing on them to make a poem of your own in the style of Captain Leechwell? The sentences are in the subjunctive. You can add to them and improve them. Be imaginative.

- If I could sail my ship through …
- I wish I could drain the oceans dry …
- I would be very sad to …
- If mermaids could dream …
- They wouldn't dare to clash swords would they? …
- She would wrap her anchor in the seaweed …
- My parrot suggested his wings could take him …
- If I were strong enough to …
- Should the stars be bright enough …
- We may take the roughest seas …

# Challenge

Lori has found evidence that Captain Leechwell was locked in prison for a few months before he escaped. She has found a piece of parchment in which every line begins either with 'If I could' or 'I wish I could'. She has no idea what the poem was because the rest of it was ripped off. Can you imagine that you are Captain Leechwell writing the poem in your prison cell. Add at least 8 more lines of your own which either begin with 'If I could' or 'I wish I could'.

If I could _____

I wish I could _____

If I could _____

**Getting to Grips with English Grammar, Year 6**

*Dogwellan Lighthouse*

# Visiting the Dogwellan Lighthouse

**Question tags** are small questions which come at the end of a sentence. They are used to check whether something is true or not. They are more commonly used in speech or informal writing. Normally we used a positive question tag with a negative sentence and a negative question tag with a positive sentence.

Craig Higgins knows a great deal about the Haunted Lighthouse. Some school children are visiting the lighthouse and are asking him questions about it. Can you add the correct question tag to these sentences?

| Positive statement | Negative tag | Negative statement | Positive tag |
|---|---|---|---|
| It was a good party, | **wasn't it?** | It wasn't a good party, | **was it?** |

The ghost's still around, _____

They did lots of smuggling, _____

They weren't caught, _____

We can see the caves, _____

They hid stuff, _____

It was haunted, _____

Benny has some questions. How do you think he began each sentence?

_____ wasn't it?

_____ couldn't they?

_____ haven't they?

_____ can they?

_____ did they?

_____ could they?

# Challenge

If you could ask Craig about the lighthouse, what would you say and with what question tags would you end the sentence?

Dogwellan Lighthouse

# Plotting at the Smuggler's Arms

Captain Leechwell is at the Smuggler's Arms Inn with his band of men. They are having a well deserved rum! Match the question tag to the correct sentence.

It was rough last night, _____

We did well, _____

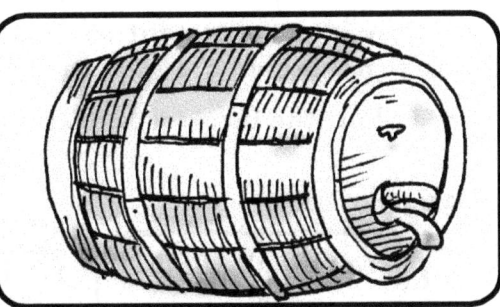

won't there?   didn't we?

have you?   can we?

shouldn't we?   wasn't it?

can't we?   weren't we?

We were lucky not to be captured, _____

We should move the goods, _____

We can hide the barrels in the caves, _____

We can't trust Jake Smiley, _____

There will be a full moon tonight, _____

You haven't got the rum, _____

## Challenge

Some of the sentences need question tags and some of the question tags need sentences before them.

I, Captain Leechwell, am one of the finest smugglers on the coast. Last night, we smuggled ten barrels of rum into the caves, _____? It was a fine haul, _____? The ship ran onto the rocks at midnight. _____, wasn't it? We tied lanterns to the goats' necks and they ran along the shore. The King's Men couldn't find us, _____? _____, can we? It was a daring raid, _____? We only just hid the stuff in time, _____? It's a hard life, _____? _____, shouldn't we?

Getting to Grips with English Grammar, Year 6

Dogwellan Lighthouse

# Contraband Calamity

**Question tags:** Positive statement = negative tag. Negative statement = positive tag. Remember to use the same verb to make your question tag, as the main part of the sentence. For example: You **are** coming, **aren't** you?
*Be careful with '**I am**' as the question tag for this is '**aren't I**'.

There's been a bit of a problem with the latest shipment of smuggled goods. Captain Leechwell is having an argument with his men.

Which question tags are incorrect? Colour the incorrect question tags blue and then correct them.

Highlight the correct question tags green.

- I couldn't help it, can I? _____
- You didn't climb it, did you? _____
- It was very dangerous, didn't it? _____
- We couldn't see, could we? _____
- Finn was nearly washed away, hasn't he? _____
- Goliath fell over, wasn't he? _____

Captain Leechwell is furious! Add the correct question tags to these statements.

- He dropped it, _____?
- You'll hide them, _____?
- He couldn't carry it, _____?
- Benny isn't a sailor, _____?
- Finn's a blithering idiot, _____?
- You're not thinking, _____?
- I am reckless, _____?
- You didn't bring the cart, _____?
- You haven't listened, _____?

## Challenge

Imagine you are one of the smugglers, write an account of the failed attempt to bring the smuggled goods ashore. See how many question tags you can use in your account.

# The Legend of Dogwellan Lighthouse

Write a story about the 'Legend of Dogwellan Lighthouse'. Use the story planners below to write notes to help you sort out your ideas first.

> A **legend** is a story that has been told through the centuries. It has things added to it throughout the ages. Legends can give us an insight into people and cultures. Legends have amazing characters who may have strange features or different powers. Usually there is a fight or conflict between good and evil.

**Use the 5 'W's to help you plan your ideas.**
who? _____
what? _____
why? _____
when? _____
where? _____

**Setting:**
The lighthouse and coastline around it. Write notes.
_____
_____
_____
_____

**Characters**
Think about their powers/strengths/weaknesses.




**Problems and Resolutions**
What are the problems? How will they be resolved?

_____
_____
_____
_____
_____

Dogwellan Lighthouse

# Mini Quiz

**A. Identify the subjunctive sentences with a tick in the box.**

1. If I were a ship at sea, I would be pleased to see the lighthouse.

2. If I were the old lighthouse keeper, I would take care of the lighthouse.

3. The lighthouse is now a national monument.

4. I wish it were possible to rescue everyone at sea.

5. I propose that the lighthouse be renovated.

6. I wish I were able to fly like a seagull.

**B. Distinguish between formal and informal writing with either an 'F' or an 'I' in the box.**

My Dear Captain Leechwell,
How kind of you to take the trouble to call. I would be delighted to accept your kind offer.
Your old shipmate,
Godly Harrington
1.

Honoured Sir,
I am in receipt of your consignment of special goods. Every care will be taken in the distribution to our respected clients.
I remain, Dear Sir,
Yours most respectfully,
Mr Huntley
2.

Hi Liz
How are you doing? Great to see you last week! Keep in touch!
Loads of love
Ashley xxx
3.

Dear Sir/Madam,
Thank you for your letter of the 18th March, 2029. We note its contents, thereof.
Yours faithfully,
Desmond Little Esq.
4.

**C. Add an appropriate question tag to the phrases below.**

You've got the goods, _____ .

It was yours, _____ .

I did do that, _____ .

That was right, _____ .

# The Wobbly Flower Show

> **Colons** are used before a **list of words**, **phrases** or **clauses**. If the items in a list are longer than one or two words, separate the list from the sentence with a **colon**.

## Wobbly Flower Show

**Saturday 16th May 2065**

A fantastic day out for all the family! Enjoy a huge range of attractions such as: sheepdog trials, specialist growers, plants and seeds for sale, Exhibitors' Tent, Morris dancers and a small, petting zoo.

Demonstrations from a variety of experts: flower arranging, propagating your seeds, rearing tomatoes successfully, container growing and lots more!

Keep the kids entertained with: popcorn, candy floss, fairground rides, falconry displays and gardening for wildlife!

Explore a wide range of reasonably priced food stalls: Hog Roast, Hot Dog Stands, Chilli Cabin, Burger Bar, Tammy's Tea Tent, Pancakes and Waffle Hut.

This year, support our charities: Cats' Protection League, Dillyford Donkey Sanctuary, The Orchid Trust and Helping Hedgerows.

**Tickets:** Adults £8
Children (8–14) £4
OAPs Free
Family ticket (2 x adults and up to 3 children) £20

**Looking forward to seeing you all there!**

---

Create a poster of your own for the Wobbly Flower Show's rival, Cobbly Flower Show, who have decided to be difficult and have their own flower show on exactly the same day as the Wobbly Flower Show!

How will you attract the crowds to the Cobbly Flower Show? What special attractions will you have? Don't forget to use colons for your lists!

*The Wobbly Flower Show*

# Colon Capers

**Colons** are used before a **list of words**, **phrases** or **clauses**. If the items in a list are longer than one or two words, separate them with a **colon**.

**Put the colons in the appropriate place in the text, just before the list. The first has been done for you.**

Melvyn Hogg is hoping to win a variety of classes with his pony Cratchett: Best in Show, the jumping, the gymkhana races and the hurdles.

Miss Sawyer has been busy preparing her competition vegetables giant spring onions, huge artichokes, beetroot and a vast marrow.

Cherry Field brought different cakes for the tea tent to sell delicious chocolate cake, strawberry meringues, lemon drizzle cake and flapjacks.

Colonel Clopper drank too much in the beer tent. He knocked over three tables a lamp two plates of sausage rolls a glass and an elderly lady.

**Make up an appropriate sentence of your own using a colon to separate a list of items. Make the items to do with the Wobbly Flower Show, and indicate who they belong to, just like the ones above. Compare what you have written with a friend.**

_____
_____
_____
_____
_____
_____
_____

# Challenge

**Cally Cooke has an advertisement for her sewing stall. Design an advertisement for Kalvin Klapp, who has a stall which sells products for dogs. Use colons (see Cally's advertisement as an example) to list his products. How many sentences with colons can you use?**

Sewing Surprise
Get busy with our amazing sewing supplies: wool, patchwork pieces, felt, colourful cottons and children's kits.
We also sell: needles, threads, scissors and pin cushions.
sewingsup@hotmail.co.uk

# Cookery Demonstrations and Dog Trials

**Semi-colons** can be used in lists to separate longer phrases.

Helga Haggis is giving a cookery demonstration in the big tent. Put the semi-colons in the right place to separate the longer phrases in the list. The first has been done for you.

| | |
|---|---|
| Today, we are going to make strawberry coulis. This is like a strawberry sauce. You can make different types of coulis: a delicious blackberry coulis; a soft mango coulis; a melt-in-the-mouth apple coulis and don't forget a raspberry coulis. | You can use your coulis for all types of things, delicious over scrunchy meringues or vanilla ice-cream use to cover your fruit pies or just dollop on top of apple turnovers. |
| To make your coulis you need a few things a solid-based pan plenty of your fresh fruit enough sugar and a strong wooden spoon. | I've got a variety of delicious things for you to try a fabulous blackberry and apple pie a delicious lemon meringue pie peach and ginger ice-cream and a beautiful custard tart. |

Stanley Ferret is giving a dog obedience class in the large show ring. Put the semi-colons in the right place to separate his longer lists.

As you can see, we've got a few trainers in the ring Wendy with the glorious little Pickle Tamsin with Bonnie the retriever and Simone with Freckles the black labrador.

I'm now going to ask Simone to bring Freckles to the centre she'll ask her to sit then he'll walk away to the other side she'll wait patiently and then she'll send her away.

# Challenge

Finish the lists for the following stall holders. Don't forget your semi-colons.

| Lydia Crumble | Brian Diggins |
|---|---|
| I've got some lovely, knitted products: | Our gardening supplies are great: |

# Super Challenge:

Can you write three more lists for three different stall holders.

*The Wobbly Flower Show*

# Wobbly Contestants and Helpers

Most action is done using the **active voice**. For example: The dragon burnt the shed down. *The dragon* (the subject of the sentence) is doing the action. The **passive voice** is used when the subject has the action done to it. For example: The shed was burned down by the dragon. The **passive voice** is not as strong as the **active voice**. It uses words such as 'was' and 'were' and 'by' to show who did the action.

**Match the active sentence to its correct passive sentence.**

| Captain Cowstick has grown the enormous melons. | The delicious Victoria sponge cake was made by Doctor Pumfrey. | The amazing sweet peas were grown by Tiffany. | The enormous melons were grown by Captain Cowstick. |
|---|---|---|---|
| Horace Flagpole has lost his dog, Bouncer. | Tamsin kissed her pony, Twickle. | Delphine is organising the sheepdog trials. | The sheepdog trials are organised by Delphine. |
| Doctor Pumfrey made a delicious Victoria sponge cake. | Twickle, the pony, was kissed by Tamsin. | Bouncer, the dog, was lost by Horace Flagpole. | Tiffany grew some amazing sweet peas. |

**Change the following sentences from the active to the passive voice.**

| Lady Wortlegrass opens the show every year. | |
|---|---|
| Ravi Gupta's giant okra won the largest vegetable class | |
| Mrs Twangle and Doctor Lint organise the tea tent. | |
| Miss Spoonfellow has grown the huge, blue carrots. | |
| Chowdry Chuppati has grown a red Snazzersnip plant. | |

# Challenge

Write five sentences of your own in the active voice about the contestants at the Wobbly Flower Show. Then change your sentences into the passive voice.

# Wobbles at the Wobbly Flower Show

Tick to say whether the sentence is active or passive. Then write the sentence out again using the opposite voice to the one you have ticked. The first has been done for you. Then write two examples of your own – one in the active voice and one in the passive voice.

|  | Active voice | Passive voice |  |
|---|---|---|---|
| Charlie, the show organiser's cat, chased a mouse. | ✓ |  | The mouse was chased by Charlie, the show organiser's cat. |
| The Chilli Cabin was broken by the tractor. |  |  |  |
| Dulcey's pot of organic heather won third prize. |  |  |  |
| The vet checked Sammy Hart's pony, Boggle. |  |  |  |
| The sheepdog trials were stopped when Brian's dog, Smudge, chased a fox. |  |  |  |
| Sarah Drubble was chased by a goat in the petting paddock! |  |  |  |
| Madge Dimweed stole Harry Porter's two metre marrow. |  |  |  |
|  |  |  |  |
|  |  |  |  |

# Challenge

**Shelly is one of the organisers of the Wobbly Flower Show. She has been keeping a log of all the items that have been lost, destroyed, ruined or gone wrong at the show. Write her notes out into passive voice. Then have a go at making your own log of disasters, using the active voice.**

Bob Dilly lost his sheep near the car park. Mae Brown ripped her blue dress. Colonel Cork smashed Mrs Mason's vase of flowers in a fit of temper. Lucy Trugg's pony, Bottle, ate Lenny Red's carrots. Mrs Owen fainted when she won first prize for her begonias. Three sheepdogs stole the sausages from the Crazy Grill's barbecue. Billy and Benny Bolt released all the petting zoo rabbits into the field.

The Wobbly Flower Show

# Flower Show Headlines

> Sentences can be written using either an **active** or **passive** voice:
> The cat (subject) chased the mouse (object) – **active**.
> The mouse was being chased by the cat – **passive**.
> Some **passive** sentences do not say who or what is doing the action. Example: The carrot was eaten.
> The **passive voice** emphasises the person or thing receiving the action.
> Good times to use the **passive**:
> - When the performer of the deed is unknown.
> - When the performer is less important.
> - When you want to position important information at the start of a sentence.

When the subject is performing the action, the sentence is active.

If the sentence is a passive one, the subject has the action performed upon it.

For example:
The <u>heavy marrow</u> broke the table. (Active voice)
The <u>table</u> was broken by the heavy marrow. (Passive voice)

| Voice | Subject | Verb | Object |
|---|---|---|---|
| **Active voice** | The heavy marrow | broke | the table. |
| **Passive voice** | The table | was broken | by the heavy marrow. |

Local papers have produced a series of headlines about the Wobbly Flower Show. Decide whether they are active or passive and discuss why with a friend. Transform each of them into the opposite voice.

- Dogs eat prize marrow
- Show jumping ring overrun by rabbits
- Gnomes steal Dahlias
- The wind blew the tea tent over in the car park
- The rosettes were eaten by the ponies
- Prize Roses Gobbled by Goats

# Challenge

Try making up five passive and five active headlines of your own!

| Active voice | Passive voice |
|---|---|
| | |
| | |
| | |
| | |
| | |

# Dog Trials

**Homophones** are words which sound the same, however, they are spelt differently and they have a different meaning!

A lot of people are trying their hand at the 'Away and Fetch' dog class.
Ollie is there with his dog Banana. Banana has to sniff out the bones and put them with the correct sentence.

- The _____ of Wight is a good holiday spot!
- All dogs should be kept away from the _____ of cows.
- Children in the Pony Parade should keep to the centre _____ in the ring.
- We _____ some gossip at the tea tent!
- Parking next to the tea tent is not _____
- A strong _____ was blowing under the tea tent's flaps.
- Please do not speak _____ whilst the show jumping is taking place. It upsets the ponies.
- The actor, Vernon Kennedy, has made a _____ copy of his speech!

Bones: heard, aisle, allowed, draught, herd, Isle, draft, aloud

# Challenge

Use the following homophones in sentences of your own:

- flower/flour
- bridle/bridal
- guest/guessed
- past/passed
- practice/practise
- steal/steel
- morning/mourning
- serial/cereal

The Wobbly Flower Show

# Village Fête

There is always a lot of talk and gossip at the village fête when all the villagers get together. Circle the correct homophone in each sentence.

1. The bakery made a huge prophet/profit due to their new cakes.

2. They went past/passed me without even stopping to help!

3. Jilted him at the alter/altar she did ... I was shocked!

4. Sally said she herd/heard barking so she went to look.

5. They had to put in a huge girder of steel/steal to keep the wall up.

6. They were stuck in the snow drift for ours/hours until they were rescued!

7. Benny was outraged! He said it was an awful television serial/cereal.

8. I said it was their/there fault.

9. He said the descent/dissent down the mountain was really steep.

# Challenge

Now use the incorrect word from each sentence and put it into a sentence of your own, to add to the gossip at the village fête!

1. _____
2. _____
3. _____
4. _____
5. _____
6. _____
7. _____
8. _____
9. _____

# Contestant Interviews

**Punctuating speech**: Speech marks are used to show when someone is doing the talking.

Some rules to follow when punctuating speech:

"What a miserable journey," groaned Yasmin. *(The speech marks open the speech and close it when the person has finished talking. There should also be a comma to separate the direct speech, so after the comma the 'g' should be lower case.)*

Franz said, "That dog is a menace!" *(The punctuation is within the speech marks. Note that 'T' needs to be a capital letter.)*

"I'm very upset," announced Benny, "this has been an awful day!" *(Because there is a comma after 'announced Benny' there needs to be a lower case 't' for the next part of the speech.)*

"I'm furious!" shouted Taj. "That was really unfair!" *(Notice that all the punctuation is within the speech marks. After the exclamation mark at the start, 'shouted Taj' starts with a lower case 's'. After a full stop, however, you should begin the speech with a capital letter.)*

**Owen McTavish is interviewing some of the contestants who have won prizes at the Wobbly Flower Show. Can you write out what they say correctly using speech marks.**

I spent weeks nurturing my peas explained Billy Hawkins. It was really worrying when we had a frost.

Faye said Beryl's cake really was amazing, she should have won. She added I do think I should have come second not third!

Caleb moaned I should have been the winner.

# Challenge

**Punctuate everything in this passage including the speech.**

Greta's pony should never have won moaned Lotty it was really unfair she knocked down the last fence and the judge ignored it I know you are disappointed soothed Lotty's Mother but you must accept the Judge's decision I think Lotty is right added Mrs Chippers it was very unfair and someone should complain Mrs Chippers looked crossly at Greta that rosette doesn't belong to you she muttered angrily it belongs to me sobbed Lotty miserably.

# Wobbly Judges

**Punctuating Speech**: Speech marks are used to show when someone is doing the talking.

The Wobbly Flower Show Judges are discussing the various flowers before awarding prizes. Turn their comments in the speech bubbles to direct speech. The first has been done for you.

**Kevin argued**: I think Denise Lumpleigh's beautiful roses should win first prize.

Kevin argued, "I think Denise Lumpleigh's beautiful roses should win first prize."

**said Shelley**: But Derek Butterby's miniature maple bonsai is stunning.

**announced Fergus Nutleigh**: I was most impressed with Meena Patel's herbs but I think Emma's daisies were gorgeous, really spectacular.

**Lenny Evans snorted**: I'm not choosing the lilies, they're nearly dead. I don't think they were given any water!

# Challenge

Write imaginative conversations of your own for the following people. Use speech marks correctly.

1. What do you think Nellie Benderby said about Colin Creeper's hyacinths?
2. What did Elda Evans say about Angie Raven's hanging basket?
3. What did Andrei Grendal say about Horace Grudge's gnome arrangement?
4. What did Dilys Davis say about Jack Jumper's daffodils?
5. What did Elsa Ribbon say about Nils Troller's begonias?

*The Wobbly Flower Show*

# Wobbly News

Imagine you are a news reporter, reporting for the local newspaper about the Wobbly Flower Show. Give a report on how well the show did and the various things people could do there. Don't forget to give your newspaper a name. Make sure you have a punchy headline and a picture. Remember your punctuation and your colons.

(Name of Newspaper)

(Heading)

(Photograph)

# Challenge

Create some advertisements for the newspaper.

*The Wobbly Flower Show*

# Mini Quiz

**A.** The Perkins Family have bought a lot from the Wobbly Flower Show.
Add colons to introduce their lists. Don't forget to use commas in the correct places too!

**Mrs Perkins**

I had a fantastic time at 'Fancy Flowers' where I bought gloves twine plastic tags plant pots a hoe and a pair of gardening shears.

**Mr Perkins**

I finally found Doggie Delights where I purchased dog treats a leather lead dog bed harness and a soft coat.

**Sally Perkins**

At the sweet shop I went mad and got tangy Twizzlers gob-stoppers chewing gum liquorice sticks chews jelly bears and three tins of fudge.

**B.** Lenny has been on the loudspeaker all day! Tick the active voice statements with a blue pencil. Tick the passive voice statements with a red pencil.

1. Sally Jones won the show jumping class on her pony Twizzle.
2. The lost dog was found by the tea tent.
3. Dog agility classes can be found in the main arena.
4. The sheepdog trials were won by Henry Harris and his dog Skip.
5. The burger bar ran out of burgers and hot dogs.
6. First place was won by Kelly with her dog Gruff.

**C.** Use semi-colons to separate the items in these more detailed lists. Then write some of your own.

The sheepdog trials were not without problems one dog chased a squirrel up a tree another went to sleep in the middle of the field two of them had a fight and Fido ran home!

There were some amazing plants and vegetables Mrs Custar's gorgeous roses the small bonsai trees the enormous courgettes and the flower arranging.

_____
_____
_____

_____
_____
_____

# Pinkton-on-Sea Newspaper

> A variety of **layout devices** can be used to set out information: headings, subheadings, bullet points, columns and tables.

A great deal goes on at the town of Pinkton-on-Sea. The local newspaper reports on many different stories. Editor in Chief Colleen Craddock and her team discuss which stories are going to be in the news that day. Write your own report for Colleen about all the rubbish scattered about by tourists.

## Pinkton-on-Sea Herald
### Storms over Supermarket

Outrage at the plans for the new supermarket escalated yesterday, when councillors announced that it would be sited on the town common.

The council offices were the scene for angry demonstrations by locals, who are opposed to the new supermarket.

"The new supermarket is totally unnecessary," local shopkeeper, Dennis Quake, told our reporter. "We've already got two big supermarkets outside town and many local shops where we can get everything we want."

Tansy Bones, the town's butcher, is concerned local businesses will be threatened by the competition of yet another supermarket. "I am concerned that this will affect all the local shops, especially the small producers who rely on the townsfolk for their business. It's already hard for them with the two big supermarkets; who undercut all their prices!"

Councillor Bob Whelks is adamant that another supermarket is necessary. "Healthy competition is always important," he announced to our reporter. "The population is growing in Pinkton-on-Sea and we need to ensure there is plenty of supply."

Locals insist that councillors have been paid off by the supermarket in order that it might site itself on prime ground within the town. "This has got nothing to do with supply and demand," local politician, Quigley Evans explained. "This has a lot to do with corrupt councillors accepting bribes."

Siting the supermarket on the town's common has incensed locals. The common is the heart of the town with its Victorian bandstand, beautiful gardens, ancient trees and manicured lawns. Conservationists worry that nesting birds, insects and other wildlife will be badly affected.

Councillors have arranged more discussions, assuring locals that these are merely preliminary talks, however, locals fear this is already a 'done deal'.

## Seagull Scandal

Seagulls have been caught on camera terrorising residents and holidaymakers.

Terrified children have had their fish and chips snatched out of their hands from marauding gangs of gulls.

"It's getting to the point where it's too dangerous to let the kids out and play," Nancy Higgins told reporters. "It's even worse when they're nesting on your chimney pot with their chicks! They've attacked us as we've tried to get into the house."

Abandoned nests have fallen down chimneys, blocking them and causing flooding.

Councillors have employed falconers to fly their hawks around the town to scare the seagulls away. Eggs have also been removed.

Gull expert, Toni "Bird Girl' Brown explained that, "Overfishing has resulted in the gulls having to seek food inland."

Residents have been warned not to eat in the open and to ensure all rubbish is disposed of in the correct bins.

*Pinkton-on-Sea*

# Pinkton-on-Sea Newspaper Planning Meeting

> **Layout devices** such as: headings, subheadings, bullet points, columns and tables, can help to make the text more readable. It can present information more clearly and attractively.

Colleen has a planning meeting every morning (very early) to discuss what will be put in the newspaper. She and her team do a big brainstorm. Here are some of their notes (which are rather messy). First sort the information within the notes into bullet points. Next - can you put all this information under some sensible headings? Looking at the content first, decide which items should be grouped together.

Break in at Freddy's Fish and Chip Shop, third break in this week to local shops. Derek's diner is closing down - it's been in Pinkton-on-Sea for 60 years. Seagull problem escalated - dog attacked and its ear gashed by seagull beak. Councillor Bobby Whelks arrested for bribery – believed to be over the new supermarket.

Thieves steal fish supplies at Freddy's place – smash rear window. Derek Dillcombe is retiring, son refuses to take over diner, daughter is in Australia. Seagull attack worsens – big vet's bill, locals frightened and worried carrying sticks and umbrellas to fight off gulls. Bobby Whelks – been having secret deals, Council offices surrounded by furious locals.

# Challenge

Reporter Sonia has been out into Pinkton-on-Sea and has brought back some new information about the seagull crisis and Freddy's Fish and Chip Shop. She has also brought back news on the increasing problem of tourist litter and some trouble with the bandstand. Imagine that you are Sonia. Write down, in bullet points, what the new information is, then write it out again carefully under some headings.

# History of Pinkton-on-Sea Bandstand

Information can be presented neatly under bold **headings** and **subheadings**. This helps the reader to find what he/she is looking for.

Local residents have been talking about the old Victorian bandstand in Pinkton-on-Sea. Here are all their comments. Sanjeet at the Pinkton-on-Sea News Station, has been gathering the information. He needs to put it under headings and subheadings. Can you help him to organise it neatly. The first has been done for you. You can put a few of the comments together!

---

**Pinkton-on-Sea Bandstand**

**Who designed it?**

The bandstand was designed by artist and architect, Grace Doolally. She was a local resident who loved sea creatures and cats. Much of her work was inspired by nature and the sea.

---

I think it was the Plumtree Creek Bridge, somewhere in Colorado, but it's not well known.

---

She was asked to design a bandstand after the Second World War. The idea was to bring music back to Pinkton-on-Sea.

---

Grace died about ten years ago. She went to America for five years to work on a bridge.

---

Derek Dingle's the band leader. Used to play the ukulele. He still does sometimes – he's brilliant at it!

---

Pinkton-on-Sea band have entered competitions all over Britain and Europe. They came second in the Tipton Bands Festival which was amazing.

---

Oh there's a lot of rivalry between the bands. There used to be stories of band members sabotaging the instruments of other bands!

---

Grace's workshop was down by the beach. It was really a converted bathing hut. She'd look out to sea whilst she worked.

---

All the band members are locals. They play different instruments: violins, trumpets, French horn, oboe, to name a few. I love their modern jazz numbers!

---

It's a funny shape, not quite round and not quite square with fancy flowers, stripes and decorations around it. There are six lamps around the top.

---

It's quite an ugly building but everyone loves it because its so colourful and fun to look at.

---

The band meets twice weekly to play. They play modern stuff, old music hall tunes, music from the movies, you name it!

---

## Challenge

Once you have gathered all your information and put it under headings, work with a friend to design a leaflet about the bandstand and its history. You can add additional information of your own and pictures.

---

It was designed by a lovely lady called Grace Doolally, a local resident. She was an architect and artist who loved cats and sea creatures. A lot of her work was inspired by nature and the sea.

*Pinkton-on-Sea*

# Seagulls

> **Subheadings** are used to separate information clearly. It gives the reader the chance to find the relevant information quickly.

**Pinkton-on-Sea Newspaper has been researching seagulls. Work experience student, Danny Deakins, has been given the job of finding out about them. He's trying to organise his subheadings. He has thought of two areas to research: Appearance and Foraging for Food, what other areas could he research about them and under what subheadings would he put this information? Use research of your own to find out more about seagulls so that you can write about all these areas.**

| Appearance | Foraging for Food |
|---|---|
| | |

| _____ | _____ |
|---|---|
| | |

# Pinkton-on-Sea Supermarket Wars

> Newspapers tend to present their information in **columns**. It is a particular style. More text can be fitted in because the paragraphs are shorter.

Pinkton-on-Sea residents are furious about the new supermarket. Danny Deakins has been given another project: to investigate the pros and cons of having another supermarket and to find out what the public would feel about it. He's got his information, he now needs to write it out as an article for the newspaper. Can you help him? You can add additional information of your own! Be creative!

**Pros**
- more competition which means lower prices
- more choice for consumers
- value for money
- closer to town so more convenient for shoppers
- their restaurant areas are good meeting points for shoppers
- they have given developing countries the chance to export their product fairly.

**Cons**
- pollutes the environment due to all the transportation of goods
- supermarket traffic generates more respiratory problems
- it is damaging the local shops and local community and putting them out of business
- to keep food fresh they generate huge amounts of packaging
- local business prices are undercut.

**Local feeling (quotes)**
___
___
___
___

# Pinkton-on-Sea Advertising

**Punctuating bullet points correctly.** This depends on whether you are using full sentences, or whether you are using fragments (not full sentences). The text that introduces your list should always have a colon at the end. For example: To hunt for shells you will need:

To hunt for shells you will need:
- a bucket
- a spade
- a hat
- sunglasses

The list contains just fragments and not full sentences, so you do not need capital letters at the start and you don't need any punctuation at the end.

To hunt for shells:
- A strong plastic bucket is essential.
- A large, metal spade will be needed for digging.
- A sun hat is advisable to keep off the sun.
- A pair of sunglasses will help protect your eyes.

In this list, the bullet points are full sentences. They should, therefore, start with capital letters and end with full stops.

**Colin Crackthorn is in charge of the advertisements for the newspaper. Can you help him with his layout?**

**Decide whether the following points should be laid out as bullet points for fragments or bullet points for full sentences. Then set them out correctly.**

To protect yourself against seagulls don't eat in public, don't drop litter, don't feed the gulls.

Yolanda's Yarns has everything you need needles, pins, fabric, wool, scissors and patterns.

The Council is committed to taking care of the elderly. To do this: we will provide support for carers, we will maintain an effective transport system and we will protect our citizens from seagull attacks.

## Challenge

Write FOUR advertisements of your own for the paper. They should be to do with Pinkton-on-Sea. Be imaginative. Two should be advertisements with bullet points for fragments, two should be with bullet points for full sentences.

# News Station Broadcast Notes

Barry hosts Pinkton-on-Sea Live, the broadcasting station, which gives live news to the residents of Pinkton-on-Sea. He puts his information into lists with bullet points. Today, however, he has been rushed. Tick the lists which are correct.

| 1. Tonight on Pinkton-on-Sea Live:<br>• more gull attacks<br>• arcade to close<br>• bus strike<br>• tourist numbers up | 2. Gull attacks have increased due to:<br>• Tourists keep dropping litter.<br>• People are still eating in the street.<br>• Tourists have been feeding the birds. | 3. New supermarket will benefit town because<br>• it will give more choice<br>• it will employ more people<br>• it will bring in healthy competition |

Barry has gathered some important information on plastic litter. Can you organise his information into lists with clear bullet points for him (like above)? Decide whether to make the list with bullet points for fragments or bullet points for full sentences.

> Different types of plastic are washed up. There are food wrappers, bottles, cups, plastic straws, plastic toys and bits of plastic fishing net.
> Sea creatures are in danger from it. They can get trapped in it, they can swallow it, they can get tangled up in it, they mistake it for food.
> We can make a difference. We can support clean-ups on beaches; we can use less plastic; tell people about the dangers of plastic and find alternative packaging materials.

## Challenge

With a friend, write out a full, detailed broadcast, imagining that you are Barry. Decide on an opening for your broadcast (something punchy and exciting to get people's attention). Add all your information from above. After your bullet point list, you can then expand on the list in more detail, just like they do on the news! For example: "Sadly there have been more gull attacks in town. Three children were badly pecked on the arms …"

# Pinkton-on-Sea Whales

**Apostrophes** can be used to show when a word has been shortened. For example: he's – he is. The **apostrophe** shows that a letter is missing.

A pod of whales has been spotted swimming near Pinkton-on-Sea harbour. Can you add the long form of each of the contractions below?

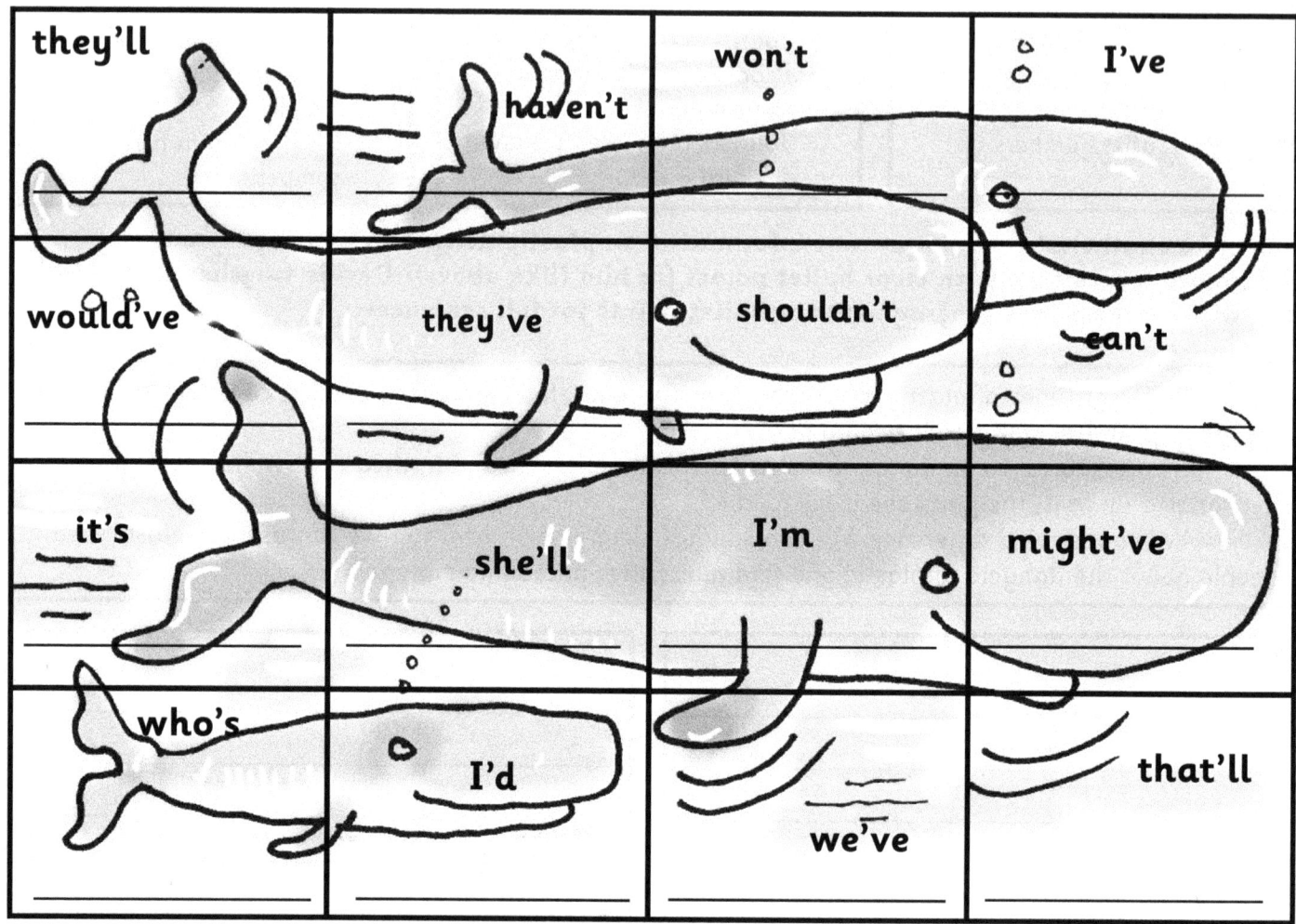

Old Kenny gives guided tours around the harbour. Make up a short speech for Kenny to give to visitors, about the harbour and the lighthouse. Use all the following contractions in the speech. Beside each one, write what it is short for.

there's _____
I've _____
we've _____
didn't _____
shouldn't _____
she's _____
haven't _____

shan't _____
I'm _____
they've _____
couldn't _____
won't _____
he's _____
can't _____

# Proofreading Problems

**Apostrophes** can be used to show when something belongs to someone or something. For example: The girl's ring (singular possession), the girls' rings (plural possession).

Danny Deakins has been asked to proofread some articles for the Pinkton-on-Sea Newspaper. All the apostrophes, to show possession, are missing. Can you help him find and correct them?

## Local School Closes

Local childrens parents were angry to see their children suspended from Pinkton-on-Sea Senior School yesterday morning. The childrens clothing was deemed grossly inappropriate by Headteacher Dennis Dimby, who sent 10 children home before 9am.

"I was washing my dogs towel when Shelly turned up at the door and told me shed been suspended from school," local Mother, Nerys McHugh complained. "I was shocked."

## Dogs dramatic rescue

The lifeboats crew went into action yesterday afternoon to rescue Mrs Browns dog Sammy. Sammy was seen scampering over the Devils Rocks when the tide came in and cut him off from the beach. "We could hear the dogs barking and Mrs Browns screaming from the cliffs above," explained Dougal McTuggurt, "so we rang the lifeboat station."

## Restaurant Owner gets Ratty

The Golden Gondola Thai Restaurant closed yesterday due to rumours about a rat infestation. "I was coming out of Bettys Bakery," explained a local resident, "when I saw the restaurants bins just topple over. To my horror, I saw about thirty rats running over them." The restaurants owner, Melvin Miggles, refused to comment to reporters. Rats droppings were littered around the back of the restaurant, where a pest control van was parked later in the day.

## Seagull situation escalates

Local childrens ice-creams were snatched from their hands by greedy seagulls and a tourists sandwich was taken. Local gulls ambushed a small dog, who was saved by his owners umbrella which was brandished in the seagulls faces. "Fluffys coat was ripped and his collar broken," explained Fluffys owner, Daisy Ipkins. "The seagulls beaks pecked his ear, they terrified him!" Customers in Cathys Cafe, were dive-bombed by the birds when they tried leaving. "It was really scary", tourist Billy Biggins told reporters. "They stole my sisters hat and threw my mums gloves into the sea. The twins pram was knocked into a tree, it was really frightening!"

# Challenge

Put the apostrophes for possession in correctly for these items and then write a short newspaper clipping for each of them.

Jemimas dog Rollo
The boats masts
The fishermans nets
Mellys souvenir shop

*Pinkton-on-Sea*

# Letters to the Editor

**Apostrophes** can be used to show when something belongs to someone or something.
For example:
The girl's book (singular possession), The girls' books (plural possession).
OR they can be used to show that a letter is missing, eg He's – he is.

Pinkton-on-Sea Newspaper gets quite a few letters from various people. Before they can be published, they have to be proofread and checked for errors by the Editor in Chief, Colleen Craddock.
Seven year old Sunita Singh has also written to the Editor in Chief.

**Plural words:** Some nouns are already plural, like the word 'people'. When adding an apostrophe, put the apostrophe after the noun and then add an 's'. For example: the people's cars. The children's games.

Dear Sir/Madam,
    It is interesting to note that the seagulls reign of terror seems to continue. The councillors obligations to protect the towns people have fallen short. We are terrorised daily.
    My childrens bike ride was ruined due to seagulls wings flapping around them and the birds screeching was terrifying. One mans ice cream was snatched from him, whilst an elderly ladys stick was knocked from her hands. Peoples homes are ruined by bird poo and litter has increased as the birds raid bins.
    Yours faithfully
    Doctor Duncree

Dear Sir/Madam,
I am writing to complain about the towns supermarket. The childrens trolleys were left lying around in the car park. My cars bumper narrowly missed one of them. Isnt it about time that the supermarkets owners took responsibility for peoples welfare. Local residents homes suffer from the parking problems whilst the petrol stations queues cause havoc on the road.
This must stop.
Yours faithfully,
Donald McDonald

Dear Colleen,
I am writing to you because my teddys blanket was stolen by the seagulls. It was in my dolls pram and they flapped down and took it. I was really scared. My brothers book bag was ripped by one gull. In the childrens playground there is a lot of bird mess. We slip in it which is dangerous. We cant swing on the playgrounds swings because the birds attack us. Why wont the council do something? Yesterday, my Dads car was attacked by them when he tried to get into Grandmas house.
Can you please do something?
Sunita

# Challenge

Can you write a letter to Colleen complaining about the things listed below. They will need apostrophes before you begin writing. They should all form part of one letter. You can imagine that you are one of the Pinkton-on-Sea Residents. Remember: letters need paragraphs and punctuation. Start and end formally.

| The towns bandstand | seagulls noise | The childrens crèche |
| dustbins rubbish | Reggies dog Rusty | Bennys Burger Bar |
| seagulls nests | peoples safety | parents terror | cars roofs |

*Pinkton-on-Sea*

# "No" to New Supermarket

**Apostrophes** can show when something belongs to someone or they can show a contraction – when a word has been shortened.

**Nelly Dimwitt has just started working at the News Station. Can you proofread and correct her article on the recent troubles outside the Town Hall – she seems to have forgotten all her apostrophes!**

Angry crowds gathered outside the Town Hall yesterday to demonstrate against the proposed new supermarket.

"Ive never seen such scenes as this before," one local told reporters. "Its an example of how strongly people feel against this supermarket. Weve got too many shops as it is, we dont need any more." Peoples hopes are lying with Benny Brown, the Mayor. "Hes a sensible man and he knows another supermarket will ruin Pinkton-on-Sea," said Shirley Rivett.

Furious locals ripped Councillor Cuffmans trousers in an attempt to stop him running away, whilst Mary Boggles car was seen driving away swiftly from the Town Hall. "Shes a stupid woman, that one!" a local butcher shouted. "Shed do well to listen to public opinion." The publics opinion was certainly being ignored yesterday as no one from the Town Hall was prepared to comment on the supermarket. The Town Halls caretaker, Ned Williams, was told to close the doors early until further notice.

The supermarkets sponsors were also unavailable for comment. "Briberys disgusting!" Maddie Oaks, a local shopkeeper, told reporters. "All these small shops will close as a result of the Councils actions. Its sheer corruption!" Ms. Oaks statement was supported by all the protesters. The problem is not likely to be solved immediately.

**Put the apostrophes into Nelly's lists.**

Councillor Cranes notepad
Bumbles Bakery
the suitcases locks
the childrens scratches
the elves day off
the Town Halls offices
Mary Boggles statement
the houses chimneys
the bandstands roof
the gardens flowers
the rabbits hutch

Freddys fish shop
the tourists litter
the Editors letters
the news stations reporters
Marys report
the seagulls beaks
the supermarkets problems
the butchers shop
the Town Halls doors
Mr Pritchards coat
the lions cubs

# Pinkton-on-Sea Carnival

Every year there is a carnival at Pinkton-on-Sea. The Newspaper has to give a report on the event. Colleen is holding a meeting of all her staff to discuss what they are going to write about this year. Make a bullet pointed list of all the dramas and events that occurred at the carnival. You can be inventive and imaginative. When you have made your list, write a full newspaper report on the carnival. Think of a great headline. Use subheadings where necessary to make your information clear.

**List of events and dramas**

**Headline ideas**

Write your report up in detail. Don't forget to use your punctuation correctly. Remember to add a picture of the carnival. You will also need some quotes from people who were there (you can make them up)! Have fun – be creative!

*Pinkton-on-Sea*

# Mini Quiz

**A. Make up an appropriate heading for the following information.**

| The gulls were spotted swooping down and snatching the rusk from the baby's hand. | Severe gales last night brought the roof of the bandstand crashing to the ground. Locals were devastated by the mess! |

_____   _____

**B. Organise the following information into a bullet pointed list. Decide if the bullet points should be punctuated for a fragment or for a full sentence.**

Sea gulls are happy to scavenge things such as food scraps, leftovers, dog food, curry, fish and chips.

Pinkton-on-Sea is a great tourist destination because it offers a wide variety of activities, it has a good base of hotels, the beach is well maintained, the children's activities are entertaining and free.

**C. Add in the apostrophes to Beryl's work to show the contractions. Then say what the contractions are actually short for.**

Ive had a great idea. Weve got some great material about sharks being sighted off Pinkton-on-Sea Sands. Its a great opportunity to write about. Theres a great deal in the news about sharks! Id happily write about it if youd let me!

**D. What heading would you give to this writing. What subheading could you also add.**

Storms prevented local trawlers from fishing yesterday, as huge waves devastated the coastline and wrecked homes, rail lines and beaches. This is another blow for fishermen whose livelihood has been badly affected by depleted fish stocks and government bans on where they can fish.

Headline: _____

Subheading: _____

**Getting to Grips with English Grammar, Year 6**
© Charlotte Makhlouf and Brilliant Publications Limited

*This page may be photocopied for use by the purchasing institution only*

# Answers

**Man-eating Shark!** *Page 15*
Hyphenated words: Man-eating, twelve-year-old, wide-eyed, fast-moving, close-up, razor-sharp, co-ordinated, in-depth, up-to-date, co-operate, open-minded, one-off, co-ordinating.

Accounts will vary but should include the hyphenated words.

**Ambiguous Headlines** *Page 16*
Man eating shark – the man is eating a shark.
Man-eating shark – the shark is a man-eater!
Whale eating fish – the whale is eating the fish.
Whale-eating fish – a whale which likes to eat fish.
Film star in high rise flat scandal – The film star is in a high up scandal involving flats.
Film star in high-rise flat scandal – the film star is mixed up in a scandal to do with high-rise flats.
Pig headed reporters annoy locals – reporters who have heads like pigs are annoying local people.
Pig-headed reporters annoy locals – stubborn/determined reporters are annoying local people.

*Challenge:* Answers will vary. Children should brainstorm as many hyphenated words as possible to start with then they can think of ways in which they can use them in an ambiguous manner.

**Twycombe Bay Match** *Page 17*
Build-up, heavy-handed, hard-hearted, wide-eyed, tight-lipped, even-tempered, long-winded, fast-moving, half-baked.

*Challenge:* Answers will vary, however, correct understanding of the meaning of the words is important and this should be reflected in the sentences made.

**Derek's Diner** *Page 18*
Noun phrases to be coloured:
  A scary grey fin.
  A huge mouth.
  What a shame!
  Some enormous teeth.
  The young surfer.
  That foolish young man.
  That horrible shark!

Noun phrases in comments:
I saw <u>a huge, grey **snout**</u> poking out of <u>the cold **water**</u>. Snout and water are the nouns.
<u>The poor, young **surfer**</u> was on <u>his ripped and battered **surfboard**</u>. Surfer and surfboard are both nouns.
<u>The hideous **shark**</u> bared <u>its ugly, rotted **teeth**</u> before swimming away. Shark and teeth are the nouns.
He slipped on <u>the slimy **seaweed**</u> and we could see <u>the terrible **tooth marks**</u> on his <u>poor **legs**</u> and **arms**. Seaweed, tooth marks, legs and arms are all nouns.

Colleen's eye witness statement:
The noun phrases are underlined:
We watched <u>the young surfer</u> riding <u>the big waves</u> until he fell off <u>his board</u>. Suddenly, <u>a huge fin</u> rose above <u>the water</u>. I screamed 'Shark, shark!', and he slithered quickly on to <u>the board</u>. I saw <u>an enormous shark</u> come out of <u>the freezing water</u> and circle <u>the battered board</u>. Bonnie growled and barked. <u>Other frightened tourists</u> ran forward to help <u>the terrified boy</u> get out of <u>the water</u>. <u>His poor legs</u> were badly bitten.

**Shark Expert** *Pages 19–20*
Adjectives will vary for the information. Some suggestions might be: This horrible shark attack has alarmed the small community of Twycombe Bay. Twycombe Bay is <u>a beautiful/lovely/delightful/pretty</u> holiday place. It has <u>gorgeous/beautiful/perfect/golden</u> sandy beaches and <u>warm/exciting/busy</u> rock pools filled with <u>quick/pretty/golden/crusty/ancient</u> crabs and other <u>exciting/amazing/interesting/beautiful</u> creatures. The <u>alarmed/worried/frightened/interested/outraged/upset</u> tourists say that the <u>enormous/huge/large/vicious/desperate/frightened</u> shark attacked the <u>poor/lonely/unwitting</u> surfer without any warning. After the attack, the <u>fast/busy/speedy/quick-response/daring</u> patrol boat was launched, but the <u>worried/calm/busy/organised/steady/capable/determined</u> sailors on it said they had no sighting of the shark. My belief is that the shark is an <u>old/crippled/ancient/elderly/injured/lost/frightened/dazed</u> porbeagle shark which had lost its way from more tropical waters.

*Challenge*: Sentences using the words will vary.

Page 20

| Time | Manner | Place | Frequency |
|---|---|---|---|
| Before we knew it, | Although I was terrified, | At the back of the boat, | Every so often, |
| Almost immediately | Even though it was a bad idea | At Porter Point, | Three times, |
| The following morning, | To my horror, | | For the remainder of that day |
| | Fast as lightning, | | |
| | As the spray lifted, | | |
| | Exhausted, | | |

*Challenge:* Use of the fronted adverbials will vary.

**Seals Attacked!** *Page 21*
(More confident children will be able to use their own fronted adverbials for the sentences. Less confident children can use the suggested fronted adverbials to help them.) Suggestions for fronted adverbials are below:

# Answers

Early this morning, I left the harbour in my small boat. Even though the sky was blue, there was a good breeze. My plan was to sail around the bay to Midnight Rock. Just before nine o'clock, I picked up Sally Barnes from the Lighthouse. For someone so inexperienced, she's a fabulous photographer. We made our way around Shingle Sands and out towards Seal Island. Amazingly, I've had my boat for twenty years! Sally was hoping to get some good pictures of the seals and cormorants. Just before ten thirty, we arrived near Seal Island. All over the rocks, we could see the seals playing. As the sun came out from behind a cloud, Sally took a few photos. To our surprise/horror/astonishment, we saw a huge fin rise out of the water! As fast as lightning/Quick as a flash/Swiftly, I turned the boat towards the island. Not surprisingly, the seals were really panicked! The waves boiled and foamed. All of a sudden/Before we knew it/Without warning, the shark burst out of the water. Suddenly, it began chasing all the seals in the water! Sally and I watched in shock! To our horror/Quick as a flash/With a twist of its tail, the shark grabbed one of the seals! Violently/ With a brisk flip, the seal was tossed into the air. We thought it was going to die! Luckily/Thankfully/Unbelievably, the seal swam away back to the island. Before we knew it/Quite unexpectedly/In the blink of an eye, the shark just vanished. Nervously/Patiently/Whilst the sun dipped, we waited for it to return. For some time/For quite a while, the seals appeared to be nervous and jittery. Unable to believe what we had seen/In total silence/Swiftly, we made our way to Midnight Rock. For quite some time, it was hard to believe what we had seen. When we had moored the boat, we reported everything to the coastguard who didn't believe us! Then we showed him Sally's photos. Accounts from the seal's point of view will vary.

*Challenge:* Reports will vary. Fronted adverbials should be imaginatively used.

### Great White Attack *Page 22*
Some of the sentences could be for a number of effects.
The boat rocked gently on the waves and I waited … pause for effect
I mean, it was a Great White … wasn't it? pause for effect
I turned swiftly, behind me two eyes glittered … trailing off into silence/pause for effect
Quickly Brian … pay attention … yes, YOU, Brian! pause for effect
Sandra get the … for goodness sakes' get it now! omission of words
And the result was … disaster! pause for effect
It couldn't be true … had they really swum this far? omission of words
"You are mine," he hissed menacingly, "all mine … " trailing off into silence/pause for effect/omission of words.

*Challenge:* For one moment time stood still, absolutely … .
We threw out the bait … literally threw it out … then we waited … .
OR
We threw out the bait, literally threw it out … then we waited …
It was a stupid idea, really stupid … but it could work.
I weighed my choices … and found there were none.
OR
I weighed my choices and found there were none … .

### Man Eating Shark Comic Book *Page 23*
Comic book strips will vary. They should include a variety of pictures and text. There should be different layouts for specific effects and the use of specific words such as BAM!, CRASH!, CRAAACCK! This sort of thing. Have a look at some comic books first of all to give the children an idea.

### Mini Quiz *Page 24*
**A.** Noun phrases: a sea snake, a small shell. Expansion of the noun phrases will vary. They should contain adjectives, adverbs and a subordinate clause.
**B.** A fish-eating sea snake. Granny wins power-driven motor boat. Two-week holidays to be won! A little-used fishing boat for sale. It's a toy-biting dog.
**C. 1)** Seriously, you went swimming … when there's a shark out there?
OR   Seriously, you went swimming, when there's a shark out there …
**2)** Get out of the water … now!
**3)** It was coming for me … run!
OR It was coming for me, run …

### Celebrity Gossip *Page 25*
Children should mark all the semi colons with a highlighter.
*Challenge:* Diary extracts will vary. They should be interesting and chatty.

### Tammy's Diary *Page 26*
I'm going to be the face of Lemonelle; they are the top beauty manufacturer!
Bonnie Tickler fell down the steps of the Okoko Club; she broke her ankle.
Had supper with Raymondo Glass who rides an old motorbike; I was wearing a short skirt so I couldn't get on it!
Colin Creedy hit a police officer outside the Okoko Club; I don't think he's enjoying the cells.
Went round to the offices of Lemonelle; what an amazing building it is. Met Gerry Rainbow; he's the photographer. We did a series of photos; he wants to get an idea of how to shoot me. Had lunch with

# Answers

Mary Lolly; she's got a new dog called Smoky.

*Challenge:* Sentences will vary. It should relate to the first part of the sentence in some way.

### Celebrity Wedding *Page 27*
I don't want the ceremony to be in a church; an open air setting would be prettier.
Lenny doesn't want it to be too formal; some people want to wear jeans.
I'm keen to avoid wearing a white dress; white always makes me look so drained!
I'd like the cake to be in the shape of a football; there could be some small sofas around it.
We want an evening meal; it will be a nice way to extend the day.
I thought we could look at colour palettes; colour will be an important part of your day.

*Challenge:* Comments will vary. Semi-colons need to be used to separate the two clauses.

### Chatkins Magazine *Page 28*
Additions to the headlines will vary. Some examples might be:
Frankie Floata's new film a Flop Sales Drop!
New Super Hero announced as Fabulous Flash!
Helga Rinkle marries Olaf Plunk Secret's Out!
Poochie Parlour Raided Fur Flies!
Twinkle Brown trips on red carpet OOPS!
Openings will vary. Suggestions for openings could be:
Pirates raid Tycoon's luxury island could this be war!
Rise in Robots will Artificial Intelligence take over?
Helga Rinkle goes red hair dye sales soar!

*Challenge:* The 6 headlines will vary. The article will also vary.

### Poochie Pampering Parlour *Page 29*
Gwenda (subject) is going to marry Ted Brown (object), can you believe it?
The paparazzi (subject) chased Tansy (object) down the street!
The high heeled shoes (subject) landed on the pavement (object). The policeman (subject) helped to pick her (object) up!
Brian (subject) had far too much to eat and he (subject) was sick outside the restaurant (object) – so shaming!
Colin (subject) shouted at her (object). Then she (subject) threw him (object) in the swimming pool!
Des (subject) threw the guitar (object) at the old woman (object) [Point out that the old woman is an indirect object]. The old woman (subject) was furious and slapped him (object).

*Challenge:* The six pieces of gossip will vary. Subject and object of each sentence should be highlighted.

### On the Set *Page 30*
Maybelle (subject) kept forgetting her lines (object)!
Casper Craven's mask (subject) got stuck on his head (object)!
One of the lights (subject) fell on the Director's caravan (object)!
The heroine's dress (subject) snagged in the car door (object).
Sasha Grekorov's arm (subject) was broken doing a motorbike stunt (object)!
Some of the cast (subject) got sea-sick on the boat (object) going to the island!
Ogre Man's costume (subject) has been eaten by Douggie the Dog (object).
A terrible storm (subject) stopped filming (object) for three days.
Douggie the Dog (subject) bit Kevin the cameraman (object).
The catastrophes for the other subjects will vary.

*Challenge:* Sentences responding to the catastrophes will vary.

### On the Set with Colin Creepe *Page 31*
How's the film going Colin; I hear there have been some problems.
So it's got nothing to do with your leading lady; she hasn't shown up!
I hear you're doing your own stunts; isn't that very dangerous?
Oh that's just gossip as usual; some lighting didn't turn up.
Shall we move on Kev; Irina has just been delayed.

*Challenge*: Sentences will vary. Examples are:
I trained as a stuntman; there's a team of stuntmen to help me if I need it.
The film sounds really action-packed; I hear you're working on an amazing aerial stunt scene.
I hear this is your last movie; the newspapers are sure you're retiring.

### Celebrity Football Autobiography *Page 32*
When I was a kid I loved ice-cream: especially chocolate ice-cream.
I was really useless at school: I could hardly read and write. Then a guy called Bruce Goalie helped me: he taught me to read and write.
I joined the school football squad when I was six: we did a lot of matches. This really helped me become a team player: you have to help your mates.
My Mother used to be a ballet dancer: she was amazing in the Nutcracker.
At twelve, I was spotted by a local coach: he was a really great influence in my life. It was at a match against Goddling Wanderers that my life changed: this was my great breakthrough.
I was signed up for the Tigers for two million pounds: this is an unbelievable sum of money. It's an honour to play for the Tigers: they're such a great team.
I'm really careful about my fitness and what I eat: a healthy lifestyle is vital for my playing.
I met my girlfriend Polly in Spain. She is really special to me.

I'd like to help local kids play football. They are the footballers of the future.
My dream is to win the World Cup. It would be a fantastic achievement.
I have never learnt to drive. I'm going to have lessons at Christmas.
*Challenge:* Independent clauses will vary about the famous goal.

## ROSCA Speeches *Page 33*
First person: A, B, E, F
Second person: C, G, H
Third person: D, I
*Challenge:* The speeches will vary, however, there should be three for each person. The acceptance speech should be written in the 1st person.

## Autobiographies *Page 34*
These will vary. They should be interesting, varied and chatty. Various forms of punctuation should be used, especially semi-colons and colons. There should also be descriptions. The children might like to plan their ideas first of all.

## Mini Quiz *Page 35*
**A.** The storm (subject)   Atlantic Ocean (object)
You (subject) Weather front (subject) Britain (object)
You (subject) Pollution (subject)   Russia (object).
**B.** Independent clauses will vary.
**C.** Clauses will vary.

## Behind the Scenes *Page 36*
Suggestions for synonyms:
adapt – change
lucrative – profitable
redeveloped – reformed
controversial – radical/profound
rapidly – quickly
expands – grows
radical – controversial/profound
desperate – urgent
embrace – accept
*Challenge:* Arguments will vary. The children should plan their 'for' and 'against' arguments to help them when writing and presenting their argument.

## Chocco Chocolates *Page 37*
The underlined words should all be antonyms (opposite) to the underlined ones. Synonyms are in bold.
Suggestions are:
Chocco Bites
Delicious/scrumptious crispy/mini-sized snacks which will leave you **begging/desperate** for more. **Covered** in thick chocolate with a fabulous inner layer of fresh, **puréed** strawberries, Chocco bites are the perfect way to **finish** an evening.
Chunkers
Feeling **naughty/wicked**, then get Chunkers, the chunky twisted bar that can be dunked in hot chocolate for a **wonderfully** delicious/great drink!

The more you dunk further surprises are **unveiled** as **assorted** flavours burst forth: caramel, vanilla, cinnamon and blackcurrant. Get Chunking!
*Challenge:* The new chocolate products will vary.

## In Hot Chocolate! *Page 38*
Synonyms and antonyms will vary. Suggestions are below. Bold words – synonyms; underlined words – antonyms.
Roger: (Furiously/Angrily/Unhappily) This is appalling/shocking/outrageous Melvyn! You can't possibly be **considering** using artificial intelligence to do all the **labour**! It would mean the loss of hundreds of jobs!
Melvyn: (Happily/Pleased/Cheerfully) Don't be **ridiculous** Roger! It's a **fabulous/great/wonderful** idea! Just think of all the money/profit we'll make!
Roger: We don't need to **remove** people, we need to **enhance/boost** our marketing! Dreamy Sweets have employed 60 more people for their factory because they're making more sweets.
Melvyn: (**Grinning**) Then they can employ some of ours when we **change/switch** to artificial intelligence!
Roger: (**Horrified**) Making our workers unemployed/redundant will bring us awful/appalling/terrible/poor publicity, Melvyn, have you **considered** about that?
Melvyn: Of course I have! The world will **approve of, admire, welcome** my decision. It means we are **welcoming/clasping/utilising** the technology of the future. Robots are the way forward. We're moving **nearer** to the future than Dreamy Sweets.
Roger: (Upset) Our employees **require/rely on** these jobs, Melvyn.
Melvyn: We won't make everyone redundant Roger. Obviously we will keep some people to **look after** the machines. Certainly we will need the engineers to ensure the robots don't deteriorate/malfunction.
Roger: (Furiously) (Melvyn … we need **improved** packaging! We should increase our marketing campaign. This idea of yours **concerns** me deeply! The workers will be furious/so upset/distraught! There might be strikes!
Melvyn: (**Angrily**)Are you saying our marketing is dull and boring? The new sweet range is wonderful/excellent/brilliant! The trials have **indicated** that children love them!
*Challenge:* The script continuation will vary. It should be laid out correctly as a play script.
Super Challenge: Arguments for and against the robots will vary. Children could research the new trends for AI and find out real information about its use.

## Chuck Chocbots! *Page 39*
You could make this activity into an actual meeting where the class need to sit down in groups and appoint one or two of the children to pretend to be

# Answers

Charlie Dellwit and take on board their comments. The groups could then reorganise their letters, change them and present them to the rest of the class for feedback.

**Chocolate Dash** *Page 40*
Clauses will vary.

**Pop the Chocolate in the Box** *Page 41*
Noun: glacier, apple, spanner
Interjection: Aaah! Whoops, Oh no!
Conjunction: and, so, because
Adjective: timid, vicious

**Packaging Problems** *Page 42*
Noun: sweets, table, queen, potion, volcano, dragon, bird, nest.
Pronoun: her.
Adjective: delicious, evil, boiling, beautiful.
Verb: melted, drank, slept, flew.
Adverb: stickily, noisily, sweetly, happily.
Preposition: on, under.

*Challenge:* The five sentences will vary. Encourage the children to be adventurous with their sentences.

**Chocbots' Chocolate Sort-out!** *Page 43*
exuberance, palatial, placement, resemblance, performance, brilliant/brilliance, important/importance, torrential, belligerent, abundant/abundance, truant/truancy, infant/infancy, facial, defiant/defiance, vacant/vacancy, significant/significance.
currency, confidence, fractious, conscious, ambitious, frequency, fictitious, independence, ferocious, delicious, emergency, innocence.

**Robot Trials** *Page 44*
Word Families: -ial, -al, -able, gram.
Good morning!
Welcome to Chocco Chocolates. I am the latest in a line of <u>potential</u> robots for the factory floor. My work will be highly <u>influential</u> as <u>programmers</u> are working to ensure I am effective. In the world of <u>artificial</u> intelligence, we are causing a lot of interest. I have a <u>special programme</u> which <u>enables</u> me to control two machines at once. I will be <u>able</u> to read complicated <u>diagrams</u>. It is <u>unbelievable</u> that this interesting, new technology will now be <u>able</u> to control a whole factory floor. My technicians believe I will be extremely <u>valuable</u> with the <u>potential</u> to increase profitability. I am also very <u>likeable</u>.
I have <u>interchangeable</u> hands that are <u>multifunctional</u>. Recent <u>diagrams</u> have shown that I have a few <u>superficial</u> problems which will require minor <u>reprogramming</u>. Last night there was an interloper in the factory who was caught trying to steal <u>confidential</u> information about the Chocbots. He tried to interfere with the wires and panels on one of my Chocbot colleagues. Interim reports show that when I am completed, it will be <u>crucial</u> to ensure my plans are safe, so that we are not stolen by <u>rival</u> companies who feel we are highly <u>desirable</u>. Yesterday, we had an important visitor who is extremely <u>influential</u>. He has a large role to play in the <u>industrial</u> world and he was keen to watch the robots in action. He wasn't very <u>social</u> because he ignored all the humans. When I spoke to him he remarked how <u>valuable</u> we would be.

*Challenge:* Reports using different words ending with -tious and -cious will vary.

**Cafeteria Complaints and Comments** *Page 45*
The paragraphs could be either mood or viewpoint. The children should discuss what they think is better and why. It opens the class up to discussion and their own opinions. They could also discuss what would change the paragraph to make it slant towards either mood or viewpoint.
"They want to get rid of …" mood
"This is just a chance for the …" viewpoint
"I remember when the factory was a …" viewpoint
"Melvyn's not interested in people …" mood/viewpoint
"We ought to be embracing change …" mood/viewpoint

*Challenge:* The report will vary.

**Production Lines** *Page 46*
Ideas will vary.

**Mini Quiz** *Page 47*
**A.** Synonyms and antonyms will vary. Suggestions are below.
Fellow Directors,
The time has come for us to <u>increase</u> our Empire! Word has come of a <u>large, important</u> factory, named Chocco Chocolates. They produce **wonderful** chocolates of **great** quality and **delicious** taste. Chocco Chocolates will **enhance** our own company which is facing financial **difficulties** and a lack of creativity. We should **begin** talks as **quickly** as possible and consider **discussions**.

**B.** Synonyms and antonyms will vary – suggestions are:

| word | synonym | antonym |
|---|---|---|
| tasteless | insipid | delicious |
| disappointing | discouraging | pleasing |
| delicious | scrumptious | disgusting |
| furious | angry | delighted/happy |
| reward | prize | punishment |

**C.** Mouthwatering, strawberry-butterscotch swirls – the ultimate in taste.
Bring romance to your life with Hearties – feel the love envelop you.
Marvellous morsels of chocolicious fun – perfect for that dinner party.

**D.** Independent clauses will vary.

# Answers

## The Haunted Lighthouse (Page 48)
"Dear Mr Higgins ..." F.
"LoriB@notmail ..." I.
"Hi Tim ..." I.
"Father was out late again ..." I.
"Sir, I write to inform you ..." F.
"Dearest Polly ..." I.

*Challenge:* The letter should be formal. Content will vary.

## Haunted Happenings at Dogwellan Page 49
I was petrified when I spied the old smuggler on the stairs. He was carrying a bundle and walked right through me. I saw men rolling their barrels up from the shore and when I turned back, they had disappeared.

The old lighthouse has been haunted for years, since I was a child. I have seen several people carrying things in and out. One minute they are there and the next they have vanished.

I was on my boat one night. The weather was dreadful. I would have crashed into the rocks if the lighthouse's light hadn't come on suddenly and lit up the rocks. I'm sure it saved my life.

There are nice ghosts too. I was out late one night and would have fallen onto the rocks if something had not pushed me back. It was as if there were hands protecting me.

*Challenge:* The guide book will vary. The children can get together into pairs or groups to work on the guide book and pool information.

## Dogwellan Lighthouse Visitors' Centre Page 50
Write ups will vary, however, here are some suggestions below.
"Welcome to Dogwellan Visitors' Centre ... " Formal
Hi! Welcome to Dogwellan Visitors' Centre! We hope you have a great time with us and find out more about Dogwellan's lighthouse.
"The kids loved the themed ..." Informal
Children will love the themed smugglers' menu with all its food attractively arranged in mini barrels.
"There's a fab history behind Dogwellan!" Informal
There is a really exciting history behind Dogwellan, with its stories of frightening Captain Leechwell. Captain Leechwell was renowned for taking the lives of many people in order to steal his contraband. He lit beacons along the coastline to force ships to crash against the rocks.
"The staff are really great ... " Informal
The staff at Dogwellan Visitors' Centre are helpful and friendly. Wheelchair access enables elderly visitors to access its facilities easily. The cafe boasts an excellent selection of delicious teas, cakes and food.

## Dogwellan Lighthouse Visitors' Centre Page 51
Testimonial write ups will vary, however, they should be in chatty, informal language.

## Leechwell's Manuscript Page 52
Subjunctive: If I were in your position ... I am recommending ... It will be imperative ... I demand that we hide the ... Fellow Smugglers, I propose that we use ... I ask that you keep your daughter ... I wish it were possible to ...
Non-subjunctive: The weather was vile ... When we arrived at the top ... I have a cunning plan ... It took a while to hide ...

*Challenge:* Sentences will vary, however, they should be in the subjunctive and they should have relevance to the smuggling theme.

## Horatio Leechwell's Poetry Page 53
Subjunctive highlighted in bold.
Come fair or foul
Thy shining light beckons.
**I wish we could turn the stars to gold**
**and flood the sea with silver.**
**If I were younger, I would risk the churn at Sharks' Rock,**
But your wise light guides me away ...
**You demand that we go,**
**I pray that we stay,**
My ship could not spare another day of endless turmoil.
Such feckless dreams
To sink my men's bones,
**Where I wish they'll never go**
In Davy Jones's locker.
The additions to the sentences will vary.

*Challenge:* Children's writing will vary.

## Visiting the Dogwellan Lighthouse Page 54
The ghost's still around, isn't it? They did lots of smuggling, didn't they? They weren't caught, were they? We can see the caves, can't we? They hid stuff, didn't they? It was haunted, wasn't it?
Benny's questions – the start to each of these will vary. Ask the children to be imaginative!

*Challenge:* The children could work in pairs or small groups to come up with some questions for Craig. It could be turned into a Drama activity.

## Plotting at the Smuggler's Arms Page 55
It was a rough night, wasn't it? We were lucky not to be captured, weren't we? We can hide the barrels in the caves, can't we? There will be a full moon tonight, won't there? We did well, didn't we? We should move the goods, shouldn't we? We can't trust Jake Smiley, can we? You haven't got the rum, have you?

*Challenge:* The start to the sentence will vary. It should make sense and pertain to the smuggling theme. Suggestions are given below.
I, Captain Leechwell, am one of the finest smugglers on the coast. Last night, we smuggled ten barrels of rum into the caves, didn't we? It was a fine haul, wasn't it? The ship ran onto the rocks at midnight. It was a horrible mess, wasn't it? We tied lanterns to

# Answers

the goats' necks and they ran along the shore. The King's Men couldn't find us, <u>could they?</u> <u>We can't deliver the booty tonight</u>, can we? It was a daring raid, <u>wasn't it?</u> We only just hid the stuff in time, <u>didn't we?</u> It's a hard life, <u>isn't it?</u> <u>We should stop by the Old Inn</u>, shouldn't we?

## Contraband Calamity *Page 56*
I couldn't help it, could I? It was very dangerous, wasn't it? Finn was nearly washed away, wasn't he? You didn't climb it, did you? We couldn't see, could we? Goliath fell over, didn't he?
He dropped it, <u>didn't he?</u> You'll hide them, <u>won't you?</u> He couldn't carry it, <u>could he?</u> Benny isn't a sailor, <u>is he?</u> Finn's a blithering idiot, <u>isn't he?</u> You're not thinking, <u>are you?</u> I am reckless, <u>aren't I?</u> You didn't bring the cart, <u>did you?</u> You haven't listened, <u>have you?</u>

*Challenge:* Accounts will vary.

## The Legend of Dogwellan Lighthouse *Page 57*
Legends will vary.

## Mini Quiz *Page 58*
**A.** Subjunctive sentences are: 1, 2, 4, 5, 6
**B.** 1 – F; 2 – F; 3 – I; 4– F.
**C.** You've got the goods, <u>haven't you?</u> It was yours, <u>wasn't it?</u> I did do that, <u>didn't I?</u> That was right, <u>wasn't it?</u>

## The Wobbly Flower Show *Page 59*
Posters will vary. They should have interesting information and lists using colons and commas.

## Colon Capers *Page 60*
Miss Sawyer has been busy preparing her competition vegetables: giant spring onions, huge artichokes, beetroot and a vast marrow.
Cherry Field brought different cakes for the tea tent to sell: delicious chocolate cake, strawberry meringues, lemon drizzle cake and flapjacks.
Colonel Clopper drank too much in the beer tent. He knocked over: three tables, a lamp, two plates of sausage rolls, a glass and an elderly lady.

*Challenge:* Advertisement designs will vary. There should be use of colons.

## Cookery Demonstration and Dog Trials *Page 61*
You can use your coulis for all types of things: delicious over scrunchy meringues or vanilla ice-cream use to cover your fruit pies; or just dollop on top of apple turnovers.
To make your coulis you need a few things: a solid based pan; plenty of your fresh fruit; enough sugar and a strong wooden spoon.
I've got a variety of delicious things for you to try: a fabulous blackberry and apple pie; a delicious lemon meringue pie; peach and ginger ice-cream and a beautiful custard tart.
As you can see, we've got a few trainers in the ring: Wendy with the glorious little Pickle; Tamsin with Bonnie the retriever and Simone with Freckles the black labrador.
I'm now going to ask Simone to bring Freckles to the centre: she'll ask her to sit; then she'll walk away to the other side; she'll wait patiently and then she'll send her away.

*Challenge:* The lists will vary. Children can always brainstorm ideas with a friend before writing them down.

*Super Challenge:* The lists will vary.

## Wobbly Contestants and Helpers *Page 62*
Captain Cowstick has grown the enormous melons.
The enormous melons were grown by Captain Cowstick.
Horace Flagpole has lost his dog Bouncer.
Bouncer, the dog, was lost by Horace Flagpole.
Doctor Pumfrey made a delicious Victoria sponge cake. The delicious Victoria sponge cake was made by Doctor Pumfrey.
Tamsin kissed her pony, Twickle.
Twickle, the pony, was kissed by Tamsin.
Tiffany grew some amazing sweet peas.
The amazing sweet peas were grown by Tiffany.
Delphine is organising the sheepdog trials.
The sheepdog trials are organised by Delphine.
The show is opened every year by Lady Wortlegrass.
The largest vegetable class was won by Ravi Gupta's giant okra.
The tea tent is organised by Mrs Twangle and Doctor Lint.
The huge, blue carrots were grown by Miss Spoonfellow.
A red Snazzership plant was grown by Chowdry Chuppati.

*Challenge:* Sentences will vary.

## Wobbles at the Wobbly Flower Show *Page 63*
Charlie, the show organiser's cat, chased a mouse. – active
(The mouse was chased by the show organiser's cat.)
The Chilli Cabin was broken by the tractor – passive
(The tractor broke the Chilli Cabin.)
Dulcey's pot of organic heather won third prize. – active
(Third prize was won by Dulcey's pot of organic heather.)
The vet checked Sammy Hart's pony, Boggle. – passive
(Boggle was checked by the vet.)
The sheepdog trials were stopped when Brian's dog, Smudge, chased a fox – passive
(Smudge chased a fox, which stopped the sheepdog trials.)
Sarah Drubble was chased by a goat in the petting paddock. – active
(A goat chased Sarah Drubble in the petting paddock.)

Madge Dimweed stole Harry Porter's two metre marrow – active
(Harry Porter's two metre marrow was stolen by Madge Dimweed.)
Sentences will vary.

*Challenge:* The car park was where Bob Dilly lost his sheep. The blue dress was ripped by Mae Brown. Mrs Mason's vase of flowers was smashed by Colonel Cork in a fit of temper. Lenny Red's carrots were eaten by Lucy Trugg's pony, Bottle. The begonias won first prize which made Mrs Owen faint. The Crazy Grill's barbecue had the sausages stolen by three sheepdogs. The petting zoo rabbits were released into the field by Billy and Benny Bolt.

**Flower Show Headlines** *Page 64*
Dogs eat prize marrow. (active) Prize marrow eaten by dogs.
Show jumping ring overrun by rabbits. (passive) Rabbits overrun show jumping ring.
Gnomes steal dahlias. (active) Dahlias stolen by gnomes.
The wind blew the tea tent over in the car park. (active) Car park has tea tent blown over it.
The rosettes were eaten by the ponies. (passive) The ponies ate the rosettes.
Prize roses gobbled by goats. (passive) Goats gobble prize roses.

*Challenge:* The active and passive headlines will vary.

**Dog Trials** *Page 65*
The <u>Isle</u> of Wight is a good holiday spot!
All dogs should be kept away from the <u>herd</u> of cows.
Children in the Pony Parade should keep to the centre <u>aisle</u> in the ring.
We <u>heard</u> some gossip at the tea tent!
Parking next to the tea tent is not <u>allowed</u>.
A strong <u>draught</u> was blowing under the tea tent's flaps.
Please do not speak <u>aloud</u> whilst the show jumping is taking place. It upsets the ponies.
The actor, Vernon Kennedy, has made a <u>draft</u> copy of his speech!

*Challenge:* Sentences will vary.

**Village Fête** (Page 66)
1. profit; 2. past; 3. altar; 4. heard; 5. steel; 6. hours; 7. serial; 8. their; 9. descent.

*Challenge:* Use of the incorrect words will vary.

**Contestant Interviews** *Page 67*
"I spent weeks nurturing my peas," explained Billy Hawkins. "It was really worrying when we had a frost."
Faye said, "Beryl's cake really was amazing, she should have won." She added, "I do think I should have come second not third!"
Caleb moaned, "I should have been the winner."

*Challenge:* The speech should be on a new line for each person doing the talking.
 "Greta's pony should never have won," moaned Lotty. "It was really unfair, she knocked down the last fence and the judge ignored it."
 "I know you are disappointed," soothed Lotty's Mother, "but you must accept the Judge's decision."
 "I think Lotty is right," added Mrs Chippers. "It was very unfair and someone should complain." Mrs Chippers looked crossly at Greta, "That rosette doesn't belong to you," she muttered angrily.
 "It belongs to me!" sobbed Lotty miserably.

**Wobbly Judges** *Page 68*
"But Derek Butterby's miniature maple bonsai is stunning," said Shelley.
"I was most impressed with Meena Patel's herbs," announced Fergus Nutleigh. "But I think Emma's daisies were gorgeous, really spectacular!" he added.
Lenny Evans snorted, "I'm not choosing the lilies." He said in disgust, "They're nearly dead! I don't think they were given any water!"

*Challenge:* Conversations will vary.

**Wobbly News** *Page 69*
News reports will vary. Discuss layout, headlines, content, straplines, pictures etc, before the children start writing. Brainstorm ideas they could write about for the Wobbly Flower Show. Discuss what will/will not be newsworthy.

*Challenge:* Advertisements should be relevant to the newspaper and to the show!

**Mini Quiz** *Page 70*
**A.** Mrs Perkins – I had a fantastic time at 'Fancy Flowers' where I bought: gloves, twine, plastic tags, plant pots, a hoe and a pair of gardening shears.
Mr Perkins – I finally found Doggie Delights where I purchased: dog treats, a leather lead, dog bed, harness and a soft coat.
Sally Perkins – At the sweet shop I went mad and got: tangy Twizzlers, gobstoppers, chewing gum, liquorice sticks, chews, jelly bears and three tins of fudge.
**B.** Active: 1, 5.
Passive: 2, 3, 4, 6.
**C.** The sheepdog trials were not without problems: one dog chased a squirrel up a tree; another went to sleep in the middle of the field; two of them had a fight and Fido ran home!
There were some amazing plants and vegetables: Mrs Custar's gorgeous roses; the small bonsai trees; the enormous courgettes and the flower arranging.

**Pinkton-on-Sea Newspaper** *Page 71*
Reports on the rubbish will vary.

# Answers

**Pinkton-on-Sea Newspaper Planning** *Page 72*
- Break in at Freddy's Fish and Chip Shop, third break in this week to local shops.
- Derek's diner is closing down – it's been in Pinkton-on-Sea for 60 years.
- Seagull problem escalated – dog attacked and its ear gashed by seagull beak.
- Councillor Bobby Whelks arrested for bribery – believed to be over the new supermarket.
- Thieves steal fish supplies at Freddy's place smash rear window.
- Derek Dillcombe is retiring, son refuses to take over diner, daughter is in Australia.
- Seagull attack worsens – big vet's bill, locals frightened and worried carrying sticks and umbrellas to fight off gulls.
- Bobby Whelks – been having secret deals, Council offices surrounded by furious locals.

Sensible headings might be: Seagull Problem, Derek's Diner to Close, Councillor Arrested for Bribery, Break In!

*Challenge:* The new information will vary. Use of bullet points is necessary. Encourage the children to be imaginative and use different information. Encourage the use of group work or working with a friend to collaborate and share ideas.

**History of Pinkton-on-Sea Bandstand** *Page 73*
Ideas for headings and subheadings will vary. Some suggestions:
Subheading: Plumtree Creek Bridge, Members of the Band Designing the Bandstand, Grace Doolally's Life.
Leaflets will vary, however, they can contain additional information made up by the children. They can also make their own pictures.

**Seagulls** *Page 74*
Headings and subheadings for the work on seagulls will vary. Children can work together to investigate and research. Encourage depth of research and clever headings and subheadings.

**Pinkton-on-Sea Supermarket Wars** *Page 75*
Paragraphs will vary. Information relating to a particular topic should be together.
A suggestion might be:
Anger over the opening of the new supermarket has increased as local concerns over its development flourish.

Local councillors believe that the supermarket will generate more competition between the various shops which will mean lower prices and more choice for consumers. On the other hand, local people believe that the supermarket will damage business for the local shops and the local community, putting them quickly out of business as their prices are undercut by the supermarket.

Councillors also believe that the siting of the supermarket, which is close to town, means that it will be much more convenient for shoppers and readily available for everyone to enjoy. The new restaurant area will also enable shoppers to meet more easily and enjoy eating out. On the other hand, local people are concerned that the close proximity of the supermarket will mean more traffic, which in turn will mean more pollution. This will mean more health issues, especially respiratory problems. Locals believe that traffic problems will increase as more people from outlying areas will come in to use the supermarket, whilst the delivery lorries will provide even more congestion.

On the other hand, the supermarket will give shoppers much more choice in their buying. Catering for people from all over the world, the supermarket will bring in more worldwide products which will appeal to different people. As a result, they will help developing countries and ensure that they are fairly paid for their produce. This will also mean that there will be more value for money for shoppers and a greater choice in what they can buy.

**Pinkton-on-Sea Advertising** *Page 76*
To protect yourself against seagulls:
- Don't eat in public.
- Don't drop litter.
- Don't feed the gulls.

Yolanda's Yarns has everything you need:
- needles
- pins
- fabric
- wool
- scissors
- patterns

The Council is committed to taking care of the elderly. To do this:
- We will provide support for carers.
- We will maintain an effective transport system.
- We will protect our citizens from seagull attacks.

*Challenge:* The FOUR advertisements will vary. Bullet points should be used in a variety of short sentences and fragments.

**News Station Broadcast Notes** *Page 77*
Correct lists: 1 and 2. Incorrect list: 3.
Different types of plastic are washed up. There are:
- food wrappers
- bottles
- cups
- plastic straws
- plastic toys
- bits of plastic fishing net

Sea creatures are in danger from it:
- They can get trapped in it.
- They can swallow it.
- They can get tangled up in it.
- They mistake it for food.

We can make a difference:
- We can support clean-ups on beaches.
- We can use less plastic.
- Tell people about the dangers of plastic.
- Find alternative packaging materials.

*Challenge:* Full broadcasts will vary. When they are finished the children can proofread what they have written and then stage them.

## Pinkton-on-Sea Whales *Page 78*

| they'll | they will | it's | it is |
| haven't | have not | she'll | she will |
| won't | will not | I'm | I am |
| I've | I have | might've | might have |
| would've | would have | who's | who is/has |
| they've | they have | I'd | I would |
| shouldn't | should not | we've | we have |
| can't | cannot | that'll | that will |

The short speech for Old Kenny will vary. Children should try to use as many of the short contractions as they can.

| there's | there is | I've | I have |
| we've | we have | didn't | did not |
| shouldn't | should not | she's | she is |
| haven't | have not | shan't | shall not |
| I'm | I am | they've | they have |
| couldn't | could not | won't | will not |
| he's | he is | can't | cannot. |

## Proofreading Problems *Page 79*

Local School Closes
Local children's parents were angry to see their children suspended from Pinkton-on-Sea Senior School yesterday morning. The children's clothing was deemed grossly inappropriate by Headteacher Dennis Dimby, who sent 10 children home before 9am.
"I was washing my dog's towel when Shelly turned up at the door and told me she'd been suspended from school," local Mother, Nerys McHugh complained. "I was shocked."

Restaurant Owner gets Ratty
The Golden Gondola Thai Restaurant closed yesterday, due to rumours about a rat infestation. "I was coming out of Betty's Bakery," explained a local resident, "when I saw the restaurant's bins just topple over. To my horror, I saw about thirty rats running over them." The restaurant's owner, Melvin Miggles, refused to comment to reporters. Rats' droppings were littered around the back of the restaurant, where a pest control van was parked later in the day.

Dog's dramatic rescue
The lifeboat's crew went into action yesterday afternoon to rescue Mrs Brown's dog Sammy. Sammy was seen scampering over the Devil's Rocks when the tide came in and cut him off from the beach. "We could hear the dog's barking and Mrs Brown's screaming from the cliffs above," explained Dougal McTuggurt, "so we rang the lifeboat station."

Seagull situation escalates
Local children's ice-creams were snatched from their hands by greedy seagulls and a tourist's sandwich was taken. Local gulls ambushed a small dog, who was saved by his owner's umbrella which was brandished in the seagulls' faces. "Fluffy's coat was ripped and his collar broken," explained Fluffy's owner, Daisy Ipkins. "The seagulls' beaks pecked his ear, they terrified him!" Customers in Cathy's Cafe, were dive-bombed by the birds when they tried leaving. "It was really scary," tourist Billy Biggins told reporters. "They stole my sister's hat and threw my mum's gloves into the sea. The twins' pram was knocked into a tree, it was really frightening!"

*Challenge:* Jemima's dog Rollo; The boat's masts/the boats' masts; The fisherman's nets; Molly's souvenir shop. The newspaper clippings will vary.

## Letters to the Editor *Page 80*

Dear Sir/Madam,
It is interesting to note that the seagulls' reign of terror seems to continue. The councillors' obligations to protect the town's people have fallen short. We are terrorised daily.
My children's bike ride was ruined due to seagulls' wings flapping around them and the birds' screeching was terrifying. One man's ice cream was snatched from him, whilst an elderly lady's stick was knocked from her hands. People's homes are ruined by bird poo and litter has increased as the birds raid bins.
Yours faithfully
Doctor Duncree

Dear Sir/Madam,
I am writing to complain about the town's supermarket. The children's trolleys were left lying around in the car park. My car's bumper narrowly missed one of them. Isn't it about time that the supermarket's owners took responsibility for people's welfare. Local residents' homes suffer from the parking problems whilst the petrol station's queues cause havoc on the road.
This must stop.
Yours faithfully,
Donald McDonald

Dear Colleen,
I am writing to you because my teddy's blanket was stolen by the seagulls. It was in my doll's pram and they flapped down and took it. I was really scared. My brother's book bag was ripped by one gull. In the children's playground there is a lot of bird mess. We slip in it which is dangerous. We can't swing on the playground's swings because the birds attack us. Why won't the council do something. Yesterday, my Dad's car was attacked by them when he tried

# Answers

to get into Grandma's house.
Can you please do something?
Sunita

*Challenge:* Letters to Colleen will vary. They should follow the correct style of writing a letter and using a formal tone. Apostrophes for possession should be correctly inserted.
The town's bandstand, seagulls' noise, The children's crèche, dustbin's rubbish, Reggie's dog Rusty, Benny's Burger Bar, seagulls' nests, people's safety, parents' terror, cars' roofs.

## "No" to New Supermarket *Page 81*
Angry crowds gathered outside the Town Hall yesterday to demonstrate against the proposed new supermarket.
"I've never seen such scenes as this before," one local told reporters. "It's an example of how strongly people feel against this supermarket. We've got too many shops as it is, we don't need any more." People's hopes are lying with Benny Brown, the Mayor. "He's a sensible man and he knows another supermarket will ruin Pinkton-on-Sea," said Shirley Rivett.
Furious locals ripped Councillor Cuffman's trousers in an attempt to stop him running away, whilst Mary Boggles's/ Boggles'/Boggle's car was seen driving swiftly from the Town Hall. "She's a stupid woman, that one!" a local butcher shouted. "She'd do well to listen to public opinion." The public's opinion was certainly being ignored yesterday as no one from the Town Hall was prepared to comment on the supermarket. The Town Hall's caretaker, Ned Williams, was told to close the doors early until further notice.
The supermarket's sponsors were also unavailable for comment. "Bribery's disgusting!" Maddie Oaks, a local shopkeeper, told reporters. "All these small shops will close as a result of the Council's actions. It's sheer corruption!" Ms. Oaks's statement was supported by all the protesters. The problem is not likely to be solved immediately.
Councillor Crane's notepad
Bumble's Bakery
the suitcases' locks OR the suitcase's locks
the children's scratches
the elves' day off
the Town Hall's offices
Mary Boggles's statement OR Mary Boggles' statement OR Mary Boggle's statement (if children feel her name is Mary Boggle)
the houses' chimneys OR the house's chimneys
the bandstand's roof
the garden's flowers OR the gardens' flowers
the rabbit's hutch OR the rabbits' hutch
Freddy's fish shop
the tourists' litter OR the tourist's litter
the Editor's letters
the news station's reporters
Mary's report
the seagulls' beaks
the supermarket's problems
the butcher's shop
the Town Hall's doors
Mr Pritchard's coat
the lions' cubs OR the lion's cubs

## Pinkton-on-Sea Carnival *Page 82*
Newspaper reports will vary.

## Mini Quiz *Page 83*
**A.** Headlines will vary, encourage the children to be clever – suggestions could be:
Rusk Snatchers!    Wind brings the Roof Down!
**B.** Seagulls are happy to scavenge things such as:
- food scraps
- leftovers
- dog food
- curry
- fish and chips

Pinkton-on-Sea is a great tourist destination because:
- It offers a wide variety of activities.
- It has a good base of hotels.
- The beach is well maintained.
- The children's activities are entertaining and free.

**C.** <u>I've</u> had a great idea. <u>We've</u> got some great material about sharks being sighted off Pinkton-on-Sea Sands. <u>It's</u> a great opportunity to write about. <u>There's</u> a great deal in the news about sharks! <u>I'd</u> happily write about it if <u>you'd</u> let me!

| | |
|---|---|
| I've | I have |
| We've | we have |
| It's | it is |
| There's | there is |
| I'd | I would |
| you'd | you would |

**D.** Headline and subheadings will vary.

www.ingramcontent.com/pod-product-compliance
Ingram Content Group UK Ltd.
Pitfield, Milton Keynes, MK11 3LW, UK
UKHW050728220625
459968UK00009B/186